BIG DEATH
FUNERAL PLANNING IN THE
AGE OF CORPORATE DEATHCARE

Doug Smith

FERNWOOD PUBLISHING · HALIFAX & WINNIPEG

Editing: Glenn Bergen
Cover Design: John van der Woude
Printed and bound in Canada by Hignell Book Printing

Published in Canada by Fernwood Publishing
Site 2A, Box 5, 32 Oceanvista Lane
Black Point, Nova Scotia, B0J 1B0
and 324 Clare Avenue, Winnipeg, Manitoba, R3L 1S3
www.fernwoodpublishing.ca

Fernwood Publishing Company Limited gratefully acknowledges the financial support
of the Government of Canada through the Book Publishing Industry Development
Program (BPDIP), the Canada Council for the Arts and the Nova Scotia
Department of Tourism and Culture for our publishing program.

Library and Archives Canada Cataloguing in Publication

Smith, Doug, 1954-
Big death: funeral planning in the age of corporate deathcare / Doug Smith.

Includes bibliographical references.
ISBN 978-1-55266-240-3

1. Undertakers and undertaking--Economic aspects--Canada. 2. Death
care industry--Canada. 3. Funeral homes--Canada. I. Title.

HD9999.U53C35 2007   338.4'7363750971   C2007-903350-4

CONTENTS

ACKNOWLEDGEMENTS 7

INTRODUCTION 8
    One Thing This Book Won't Tell You 9
    Why Do Most of Us Know So Little about the Deathcare Industry?....... 10
    The Origins of This Book 11

PART ONE
BIG DEATH IN CANADA / 13

1.   THE INVENTION OF THE TRADITIONAL FUNERAL 14
    Death in Canada 20
    A Family Business.. 22
    Professionalizing the Funeral Director.. 22
    A Community-based Business.. 25
    Growing Up in a Funeral Home 27

2.   FUNERALS WITHOUT FINS.. 30
    Cremation 31
    Cremation in Canada.. 34
    Memorial Societies.. 35
    Cremation Catches Fire... 37
    Bringing the Finless Funeral to Winnipeg 38
    Starting Over 41

3.   FROM THE FAMILY BURIAL GROUND
    TO THE MEMORIAL GARDEN 47
    The Rural Cemetery 49
    A Case Study: The Mount Royal Cemetery...................................... 49
    Lawn Cemeteries 51
    The Modern Cemetery Industry 53

4.   BIG DEATH COMES TO TOWN 55
    SCI and the Loewen Group: A Struggle to the Death............................ 55
    A Prairie Boy's Brush with Death and Success 59
    Big Death's Tight Grip 65
    The Casket Makers... 66

5.   INVENTING NEW FUNERAL TRADITIONS 72
    The Green Funeral... 74
    Promession... 78
    Memorial Societies and Cooperatives... 78
    A Cooperative Approach 81

6. **"IF IT ISN'T ETHICAL, IT PROBABLY ISN'T GOING TO BENEFIT THE CONSUMER": REGULATING THE FUNERAL INDUSTRY** **83**
    The Funeral Rule 83
    Ontario Reforms Its Funeral Laws — Very Slowly................................... 85
    The Coming Battle Over Scattering... 88
    Regulation in a Small Province 90

PART TWO
FUNERAL PLANNING IN THE
AGE OF CORPORATE DEATHCARE / 93

Let Your Family Know What You Want... 93

7. **LITTLE NORM MEETS BIG DEATH** **95**

8. **FUNERAL DIRECTORS: AN INTRODUCTION** **102**
    What Can a Funeral Director Do for You?... 102
    Licensing and Education 102
    Industry Trends 103
    Do You Have to Use a Funeral Director?.. 104
    Death and Paperwork.. 105
    The Story of a Lay Funeral Director.. 106

9. **GIVING IT ALL AWAY: ORGANS, TISSUES AND WHOLE-BODY DONATION**.. **109**
    Organ and Tissue Donation 109
       Deceased Donors 110
          How to Become a Donor... 111
          The Donation Process 112
    Getting into Medical School 113

10. **BODY AND SOIL: FINAL DISPOSITION AND MEMORIALIZATION** ... **117**
    Earth Burial.. 117
       Will You Be Embalmed?... 118
          The process 119
       Will There Be a Visitation or Viewing? 120
       Where Will You Be Buried? 120
          Telling Your Lot from Your Plot 120
          Perpetual Care... 121
          Double Depth 121
          Interment Rights... 121
          Permanency... 122
       What Will You Be Buried In?... 123
          Metal Caskets 123
          Wooden Caskets.. 123
          Cloth-covered Caskets 123
          Casket Linings... 124
          Direct-sale Casket Dealers.. 124

Do You Need a Grave Liner or Vault for Your Casket? 124
    Grave Liners 125
    Vaults 125
How Will Your Grave Be Marked? 126
    Virtual Memorialization 126
What Are the Costs Associated with Burial? 127
    Potential Earth Burial Costs 127
    Funeral-home Costs 127
Entombment in a Mausoleum 128
    Cemetery Costs 128
    Memorial Costs 128
Cremation 130
    What Do You Wish to Happen before Cremation? 130
    Where Do You Wish to Be Cremated? 131
    What Do You Wish Done with Your Ashes? 131
        Scattering 132
        Preservation in an Urn 132
        Burial in the Earth 133
        Inurnment in a Columbarium 134
        Memorialization in a Structure in a Cemetery 134
    How Much Might You Expect to Pay for a Cremation? 135
        Funeral Home Costs 136
        Cemetery Costs 136
        Memorialization 137

11. A SERVICE TO HONOUR THE DEAD **138**
    What Is a Service? 138
        Religious Services 139
    Where to Hold a Service 139
    Inventing a Funeral Service 140
        Reception 141
    Obituaries and Death Notices 142
    Over-planning 143

12. PAYING FOR YOUR FUNERAL **144**
    Who Pays for a Funeral? 144
    What Benefits Are Available to Help Pay for a Funeral? 144
    When Should You Pay for a Funeral? 145
    The Benefits of Pay Now, Die Later 145
    How Can You Prepay? 145
        Guaranteed Items 146
        Non-guaranteed Items 146
        Financing Through a Trust Fund 146
        Financing Through an Insurance Company 147
        Pre-need insurance 148
        Whole life insurance 148

What Are the Disadvantages of Pre-buying Your Funeral? 149
    Pre-buying What You May Not Need 149
    Pre-buying Makes It Harder to Change Your Funeral Plan 149
    If You Buy Too Far in Advance,
    You May Lose Track of the Purchase 149
    The Funeral Home May Change Ownership and Philosophy 150
    When You Prepay, You Are Paying
    Now for a Product That You Will Never See 150
    You Will Not Have Access to Money That You Could Otherwise
    Spend on Yourself and Your Family While You Are Alive 150
    The Money May Not Be There 150
    The Commissioned Sales System Is Open for Abuse 151
    Pre-buying Can Create a False Sense of Security 152
       Saving for it yourself may be more effective 153

13. PREPARING A FUNERAL PLAN **154**
    How To Plan Your Funeral 154
    Prepare and Discuss Your Plan! 154
    Visit at Least One Funeral Home 154
    Choose a Cemetery — and Marker 155
    Changes in Your Plan 155
    My Funeral Plan 156
    Part 1: Donation for Medical Education or Transplant 156
    Part 2: Cremation or Earth Burial 157
    Part 3: Cremation 157
    Part 4: Earth Burial 158
    Part 5: A Service 158
    Part 6: A Funeral Service — with My Body Present 159
    Important Information about You 160
    Checklist of More Things to Do 161
    What To Do after You Have a Plan 161
    Collect Your Information 162
    Topics 162

APPENDIX **163**
    Funeral Regulators 163
    Transplant Programs in Canada 165

NOTES **166**

ACKNOWLEDGEMENTS

THIS BOOK WOULD NEVER HAVE BEEN written were it not for Norm Larsen's dedication, hard work and encouragement and Neil Bardal's cooperation and good humour. I cannot thank them enough. I also owe a significant debt to the many people who spoke to me about their experience of and involvement in the deathcare industry. I also wish to thank my daughter Erica, who read and commented on the manuscript. Finally, thanks to everyone at Fernwood Publishing, particularly Wayne Antony and Beverley Rach for their editorial and production work, John van der Woude for his cover design, and Glenn Bergen for his thoughtful editing.

While their works are cited in the footnotes, I would like to acknowledge my debts to the following writers: James J. Farrell, Gary Laderman, Herbert C. Northcott, Donna M. Wilson, Stephen R. Prothero, Brian Young, Xavier Cronin, Erick Larson, Robert Bryce, Miriam Horn, Peter Franceschina, Rafael A. Olmeda, Jonathan Harr, David Barston and Monica Davey, Seth Lubove, Michael Salisbury, Emma Cook, Paul Brown, Kenneth V. Iserson, Darryl J. Roberts, and Ernest Morgan.

INTRODUCTION

THIS BOOK IS NOT ABOUT DEATH AND DYING. It sidesteps all the big moral, philosophical, cultural and emotional questions that arise from the fact that nobody gets out of here alive. It is not even about how to arrange a funeral that will ease the grieving process and help bring about closure. In the face of death's powers, it is silent.

My goals are much more modest. The first is to outline the range of options that are available when it comes to planning our own funerals or arranging the funeral of someone else. The second goal is to provide some consumer information about how to avoid over-paying for a funeral. Finally, the book attempts to survey of the development of the deathcare industry in Canada, albeit from a regional perspective.

If you believe that cost is no object when it comes to a funeral for you or your loved ones, then read no further. There is a whole industry out there that is ready to help you plan your funeral. It is slick, aggressive and all en-compassing. It is so skilled that when it is through with you, you will have paid in advance for products and services that will not be delivered in your lifetime, in the process reaping a tidy profit off your fear and guilt. If you do not leave any funeral plan, there is a good chance that your family members may find themselves manipulated into buying fairly expensive goods and services that may well leave them feeling violated. For example, a friend of mine is still shaking his head over the fact that crowd control was among the items listed in the invoice for the funeral of his father — a pleasant enough man, but one who lived a life of quiet anonymity and drew no crowd, either boisterous or well-behaved, to his funeral.

However, if you and your family would like to maintain some control over one of the most important stretches of rough passage in a family's history, and meanwhile control expenses, then it would not hurt to know something about the structure of the deathcare industry, to know something about your options and, on the basis of this information, to prepare a funeral plan.

This is a longish book, but, I hope an interesting and useful one. The story I will tell you is not complicated. The funeral business has been largely taken over by funeral corporations, and funerals more and more resemble just another commodity to be purchased. But there are a few simple guidelines to avoiding the distressing implications to this trend:

- Pre-planning is useful. It makes you aware of options and also helps you identify what you do not what to see done. It is most effective if you share your plan with the family members who will have to put it into effect. Filling out the funeral plan form found at the back of this book will allow you to identify and address most of the key issues.

- Prepaying is, in most cases, a bad investment.
- Corporate funeral homes are usually more expensive than independent funeral homes. But one should also be wary of discount funeral homes that offer deals that are too good to be true, since their advertised prices may not include certain necessary expenses.
- Corporate cemeteries are usually more expensive than municipal and other non-profit cemeteries.
- Funeral directors are not the enemy; they can provide many important services on your behalf.
- Simplicity and dignity are closely related.

I would also note that while this book makes some critical comments about the practices of the funeral industry and corporate funeral homes, these practices are usually quite legal. Finally, I would add that most of the criticisms in this book focus on the urban, as opposed to the rural, funeral industry.

None of this, of course, will make death and dying less tragic or painful.

ONE THING THIS BOOK WON'T TELL YOU

Much of this book is about money and funerals, but it will not tell you much about funeral costs. It is one of the first questions people asked when I mentioned I was researching a book on funerals and funeral planning. Numerous books and articles quote the figure of $10,000 as the average price for a North American funeral, but I have yet to see a citation for the figure (or an explanation of what the price does and does not include). The real answer, unfortunately, is that it all depends.

First of all, it depends on what you mean by a funeral. When most people ask that question they usually are thinking of the total cost of all the services and goods that must be paid for when someone dies. But the deathcare industry has traditionally distinguished between the services provided by a funeral home, a crematory and a cemetery. So when someone says that the average price of a funeral in Canada these days is $5000 (as some people do) they are likely referring to the cost of embalming, a casket, a viewing and a funeral service, but they are not including the cost of a burial plot, digging the grave or buying and installing the marker. Put together, these latter items could cost as much as the funeral.

The cost of a funeral also depends on how you are disposing of the body. For seven or eight hundred dollars one can simply pay to have a body cremated and then scatter the ashes in the backyard, while for $10,000 you might be able to buy a niche in a columbarium where the ashes will supposedly be stored permanently. (Don't feel bad if you do not know what a columbarium is — it is essentially any storage space that is reserved specifically for holding cremated remains.) In short, the cost of a funeral all depends on what you are buying.

But if the idea of an average cost of a funeral is fairly meaningless (and as a call to Statistics Canada confirmed, currently unavailable), there is no disputing the fact that funerals can be pricey. For many years it was said that, after a car and a house, a funeral was the third-most expensive purchase a person would make. Today the price of some computers and home-enter-tainment systems might outstrip the cost of many funerals, but there is no doubt that they can still be big-ticket items.

WHY DO MOST OF US KNOW SO LITTLE ABOUT THE DEATHCARE INDUSTRY?

There are a number of very good reasons why death is a stranger to most Canadian households. Canadian life expectancy is continuing to increase, in 2003 reaching an all-time high of 79.9 years. Women continue to outlive men, with a life expectancy of 82.4 years compared with 77.4 for men. However, men have slowly closed the gap, which was 7.4 years in 1979. Statistics Canada also indicates that the number of years that a person can expect to live past the age of 65 increased to 17.4 years for men and 20.8 years for women.

The two most prevalent causes of death in Canada over the past twenty-five years have been diseases of the circulatory system (heart disease and vascular diseases, such as hardening of the arteries) and cancer, accounting for 62 percent of deaths in 2003. Circulatory system diseases were responsible for 47.3 percent of the deaths in 1979 and were down to 32.8 percent in 2004. Cancer was up from 22.9 percent in 1979 to 29.2 percent in 2003.[1]

While death can come at any time, in Canada it is affected by the seasons, with death more likely to take place in the winter than the summer. And hospitals remain the likely place for death to occur: in 2003, 67.5 percent of deaths took place in hospital.[2]

One of the reasons we are not dying at home is that we are not dying as infants or being cut down in the prime of life by an epidemic (knock wood). Families turn to professionals to bury their dead for many reasons, the prime one being the fact that almost every service in our society has been com-mercialized and commodified. But as families have gotten smaller and lives longer, death has ceased to be a regular visitor to most Canadian households. Funeral directors say that most families have to arrange a funeral every fourteen years, but that figure masks the reality of the situation. Since most of us assist in the arrangement of the funerals of parents, whose deaths are likely to be relatively close together, the time between the funerals that we are responsible for is likely to be several decades.[3]

THE ORIGINS OF THIS BOOK

This book originated in a chance meeting in the Winnipeg airport in the summer of 2005 where I bumped into Norm Larsen, a retired Winnipeg lawyer. He confided that he had been thinking of giving me a call since he had an idea for a book he thought I should write. I had come to know Norm fifteen years earlier when I was writing a biography of Joe Zuken, a long-time Winnipeg politician and Larsen's former law partner. In his retirement from the legal profession (Norm had variously served at the head of Legal Aid Manitoba, taught at the University of Manitoba law school and worked as a legislative drafter), he developed a guide to funeral planning and gave presentations on funeral planning to various community organizations. Through this work he had concluded that there was no Canadian book that dealt with the issues surrounding funeral planning.

Over a subsequent breakfast, Norm told me of how a decision to attend the annual meeting of the Funeral Planning and Memorial Society of Manitoba had morphed into a research project into the funeral industry. Through that project, he interviewed twenty-one Winnipeg funeral directors, made countless visits to funeral homes and cemeteries and wrote a detailed guide to funeral planning. "I always attend a funeral home open house," he told me. "You always learn something new." He wanted me to help turn his research into a book so that he could turn his time to new endeavours.

Through his research, Norm developed a good relationship with Neil Bardal, a third-generation Winnipeg funeral director and, as I was to learn, a maverick in the Winnipeg funeral scene. Neil, he said, had provided him with some valuable insights and would likely be willing to cooperate on a book about the funeral industry.

Bardal was everything Norm said he was: iconoclastic, big-hearted, engaging, garrulous and reflective. He understood the industry's history, was proud of his profession and anxious about the direction that it was headed. He joked about having regularly turned down purchase offers from the giant deathcare corporations that are consolidating their hold over the funeral industry. The corporations, he would say, had no imagination, no taste for innovation, no broad vision. Neil's vision was nothing if not broad. His office was arrayed with memorabilia reflecting his wide range of interests — an organ in one corner, photos of Neil with various Icelandic officials on the walls, an antique globe and books galore. Once in conversation, he casually quoted Shelley's poem "Ozymandias," to prove the point that there is such a thing as permanent memorialization.

I attended one of Norm's funeral-planning sessions, interviewed him on a number of occasions and read the detailed and often comic diary he had kept of his researches into the funeral industry. For several months I also met regularly with Neil and explored the world of the deathcare industry. Neil spoke about his family's history, giving me a detailed overview of the development of what has come to be known as the "traditional funeral" in Canada and also his own reaction to what he saw as the shortcomings of the traditional approach. I visited a number of other independent funeral homes, and when the corporate funeral homes contacted me through mail or telephone surveys, I responded and was invited out for meetings with their sales representatives. In the latter events, I simply portrayed myself as a potential customer — which, I am afraid to say, I am. I also carried out additional research into the history and structure of the North American deathcare industry, meeting regulators, memorial society representatives, funeral directors past and present and a historian of the Canadian cemetery industry.

The result is this book, which has been conceived in two parts. Part One is a story of the rise of a new profession in North America, that of the undertaker, telling how carpenters, wagoneers and furniture makers eventually became funeral directors. I have used the story of the Bardal family to illustrate this history, showing how the family improvised its way into the profession and became one of its pillars, only to produce one of its staunchest critics. There is another thread to this story: the alternative to what might be called "Big Death" — a handful of transnational corporations that control cemeteries and funeral homes, while usually trying to give the impression that they remain family-owned businesses. This consolidation has taken place over the last decade, all in anticipation of 2016, when the first baby-boomer turns seventy and the golden age of death begins in earnest. But there are alternatives to a big-death funeral on the horizon — green funerals, memorial societies and funeral home cooperatives — that, along with much-needed closer regulation of the industry, mean that funerals can be more than good for business. These chapters are meant to give readers a sense of the risks that they face in the funeral market today and why they and their family might benefit from doing some funeral planning.

Part Two is a survey of the key elements of funeral planning: the role of the funeral director, donating all or part of your body, final disposition of the body, memorialization, funeral services and financing. These chapters are meant to be assistance both in preparing your own funeral plan or in serving as a resource if you have to arrange someone's funeral. Part Two concludes with Norm Larsen's brief form for preparing a funeral plan.

As anyone who reads this book will be able to tell, it owes a tremendous debt to both Norm Larsen and Neil Bardal. They laid the spadework (literally and figuratively), provided valuable assistance and guidance, and read and commented on the manuscript. They proposed corrections, but never tried to interfere. If this book entertains, instructs or assists in anyway, it is a reflection of their efforts and understanding.

PART ONE

BIG DEATH IN CANADA

CHAPTER 1

THE INVENTION OF
THE TRADITIONAL FUNERAL

IN 1983 THE ONTARIO FUNERAL SERVICES Association (originally known as the Embalmers' Association) celebrated its one-hundredth anniversary with a gala at Toronto's Harbourfront Hotel. At what was meant to be an upbeat affair, Winnipeg funeral director Neil Bardal, one of the featured speakers, created no small amount of controversy. A graduate of the Toronto-based Canadian School of Embalming, a founder of the Western School of Funeral Service and the author of a history of the Funeral Service Association of Canada, Bardal's roots in the industry went back two generations. A big man with a friendly style and a sharp wit, he was often the industry candidate to debate its never-ending series of critics, particularly the remains-scattering cremationists (derided by funeral directors as "bake and shakers") and memorial-society zealots appalled by what they viewed as the ostentation that had come to characterize a once-severe religious ceremony. According to Bardal, "I was the industry darling — people knew my family. I had gone to school in Ontario, started my career there. I always used to praise their school and their approach to training."

Some of the people in the audience that day in Toronto were aware that Bardal was entertaining some new ideas. Three years earlier he had sold his shares in the family business and set up a new funeral home in, of all places, a strip mall. But these stories from the West had not prepared the audience for the heresy that was to come. Bardal's message was simple and apocalyptic: the traditional funeral — which included embalming, a several-thousand-dollar casket, a family viewing the night before the funeral, a funeral service with the body and the casket present in the funeral home's chapel and a motorcade procession led by a hearse and several limousines from the funeral home to the cemetery — was, he said, on its last legs. Given that the traditional funeral was the industry's bread and butter, this was a bleak message, but it was not news. Even the most change-resistant funeral director could see that the cremation rate was rising. The challenge for the industry was how to make its peace with these new developments. The most common response had been to incorporate cremation into the traditional funeral. If customers could be convinced of the need for a viewing before the cremation, there was an opportunity to embalm the deceased and sell the family a viewing casket. Or one could simply sell them a casket in which the body would be cremated. All of which could be followed by a funeral service in the chapel. And there was no reason for an urn to be a simple piece of low-cost pottery. With a little imagination and marketing skill, urn prices could even match or surpass the price of a low-cost casket.

But this is not what Neil Bardal was talking about when he spoke of the need to innovate. "I told them we had to go back to our roots," says Bardal, "to focus on caring for the body and not selling product. I got booed off the stage. When my wife and I sat down for the luncheon, people who had been my friends got up from the table and left. They would not sit with us." He felt that he had done nothing more than identify the issues that scared everybody in the industry, but instead of ignoring them, he had said the time had come to confront them creatively.

And so the funeral industry's fair-haired boy became an apostate. At the following year's convention of the Funeral Services Association of Canada, he found himself under fire from the editor of the *Canadian Funeral News*, who described Bardal as a disappointment to the industry and his family. Long an active member of provincial and national funeral directors' organizations, he soon discovered he was being sidelined. Says Bardal, "I would get letters saying, 'we can tell by what you are doing that you would no longer wish to be involved with us, therefore we are removing you from our board.'" He even lost his position as editor of the Manitoba Funeral Service Association newsletter. Twenty-five years later, Bardal runs a successful independent funeral home in Winnipeg. His son Eirik was vice-president of the Manitoba Funeral Directors' Society in 2006, but Neil says the funeral establishment still wants nothing to do with him or Eirik. Says Bardal, "When I go into a meeting with them, they want to know 'What is he going to do now?' When I talk about environmentally friendly burial, they say 'God, he is at it again.'"

Neil Bardal describes the past quarter-century, during which he rebuilt a family business on what amounts to revolutionary principles for the funeral industry, as the great journey of his life. But that journey is best understood in context of his family's history in North America and the growth of the Canadian funeral industry.

The 1873 eruption of the volcanic Mount Hecla in Iceland destroyed miles of pasture and precipitated a large-scale emigration of Icelanders to Manitoba's Interlake region. In 1875 the first Icelandic settlers began carving out New Iceland on the shores of Lake Winnipeg. By 1901 over 2500 Icelanders had come to Manitoba, and the town of Gimli, on the shores of Lake Winnipeg, was the centre of Icelandic life in Manitoba. Among these immigrants was Arinbjorn Sigurgeirsson Bardal, a young man who left the family sheep farm in northern Iceland in 1886. He was following the footsteps of his brother Pall, who had come to Minnesota in 1878. Arinbjorn made for Winnipeg, and within a few years his brother Halldor and sisters Ingunn and Asdis emigrated to Manitoba. Winnipeg was only a dozen years old when A.S. (as everyone called him) Bardal arrived to find a frontier town with grand ambitions to be the Chicago of the North. While he came to North America with few skills and little education, A.S. was determined to make his mark in the community. Like many immigrants today, A.S. wound up in the transportation business. The automobile, the streetcar and paved roads were still in the future; anyone with a horse and wagon could become a carter. With the acquisition of a hansom cab, Bardal expanded into the taxi business.

From there, strange as it may seem, it was but a short step to the funeral business. It was a transition that took place across North America in the late-nineteenth and early twentieth century. For example, Daniel and Lawrence Guymer immigrated to western Canada from England in 1909. When their attempts to farm near Tisdale, Saskatchewan, failed, they moved to the northern Manitoba frontier town of The Pas. While the brothers initially worked on local construction projects, they quickly identified a local unfulfilled need — emptying and disposing of the contents of the town outhouses. To do this they needed a wagon and a team of horses, and once they were so equipped they branched into the transport business, winning contracts for mail and liquor deliveries. When a local resident died, Lawrence Guymer, who had some carpentry skills, would build a coffin, and the brothers would use their wagon to transport it and the body to the town graveyard. Sensing an opportunity, Daniel trained as an embalmer. By 1914 their business card read "Guymer Bros. Undertakers, draymen and contractors, Agents for the Imperial Oil Company."[1]

Like the Guymer brothers, the first undertakers in most North American communities were carpenters or wagoners who were diversifying their product line. For example, Vancouver's first funeral director, Frank W. Hart, was originally a furniture factory owner. So it was that in 1894 A.S. Bardal went into the funeral business with another Winnipegger, Bert Gardiner. According to Bardal family lore, A.S. had the horses and Gardiner had a hearse, essentially a covered wagon that could hold a coffin. They worked together on an as-needed basis, with each of them drawing clients from distinct ethnic and religious groups. Gardiner's clients were largely of British ancestry, while Bardal's were Icelandic and Lutheran. Gardiner had an office on Main Street, while Bardal had a small building on Nena Street (now Sherbrook Street) that was the headquarters for his taxi, cordwood, hauling and funeral business.

When A.S. Bardal went into the undertaking business, funerals were amateur, homemade affairs, usually organized by family and friends, possibly with the assistance of a local clergyman. The preparations took place at home.

The body might be laid on a board placed between two chairs, with a forked stick wedged between the chin and breastbone to close the mouth and two coins laid on the eyelids. When it had been wrapped in the winding sheet or shroud, the body would be placed in the traditional six-sided coffin supplied by a local carpenter, usually a furniture dealer. At the funeral service, often held in the home, the minister might read scriptural passages that bore home the message that death is the wages of sin. Following a brief viewing, possibly in the family yard, the funeral party proceeded by horse and wagon and on foot to the graveyard.[2] There the coffin would be lowered into the grave that the church sexton would have arranged to be dug in advance. Family and friends would then fill the grave with dirt. The role of the undertaker was limited to picking up the body, placing it in a casket and transporting it to the church and then the cemetery.

In her autobiography, novelist Laura Goodman Salverson, who was born in Winnipeg in 1890 into a Scandinavian family, recounted her memories of the funeral of her baby brother. She wrote:

> When I slipped into the small parlour (which was, of course, no real parlour such as the minister had, but just the room where mamma's chest of drawers, her black rocker, a braided mat, and a table with flowering plants gave an air of mild formality) and had shut the door behind me, I beheld a thing that made me rub my eyes. In the middle of the room, supported by two chairs, was the loveliest white bed. I assumed that it was a bed, although so tiny and narrow, for little brother was sleeping in it.

Shortly after came a knock on the door. It was A.S. Bardal:

> A big man in frock coat entered with his hat in his hand. He nodded at papa, and, bowing a little, addressed mamma in a kind, solemn voice.
>
> "I wish I were here on a brighter errand," he said, "that there was something I could say — but what are words? It is hard — hard."
>
> "Thank you, Mr. Bardal," mother answered, in a cold small voice. "We are ready as you see."
>
> We went out and there at the door stood a hack with two black horses switching their gleaming tails. "Papa — papa," I whispered in rising elation that instantly died when he touched his lips for silence. It was all beyond comprehension. Here were we, who never went abroad in style, about to ride forth in a fine carriage such as the rich folk used for pleasure, and not one word of joy to be said. One by one

we climbed in and took our places, and then — astonishingly true — the tall stranger brought out little brother's bed, now completely covered with a crinkly velvet lid, and set it between us. Then the horses were off, stepping daintily as ladies over the rutted road.[3]

By the early twentieth century, this sort of funeral was passing out of fashion. The future lay in embalming and establishing your own funeral home, complete with chapel. A.S. Bardal had not been in business long when he and Gardiner travelled to Chicago to train as embalmers. As historian Gary Laderman writes,

> The true anchor of the American [and by extension the Canadian] way of death was the visible, embalmed body, put on display either before or during the religious service. According to morticians, the people wanted to see their dead relations one last time, and they were the only ones qualified to give them what they wanted.[4]

Embalming was key to the undertaker's claim to professional standing, since it was seen as an innovation and a scientific service. Prior to the U.S. Civil War, embalming had been a fairly invasive process that was used almost solely to prepare corpses for medical schools to use in anatomy classes. Dr. Thomas Holmes, with prior experience as a doctor and coroner's assistant in New York City, emerged during the Civil War as a founding figure of modern embalming, having helped develop effective embalming fluids, technologies and techniques that would allow the Union dead to be sent back for their families for a final viewing and interment.[5] The process got its next big push from the manufacturers of embalming fluid, whose travelling salesmen offered short — often only a few hours in length — training sessions on how to use their new products. A former casket salesman, Joseph H. Clarke, established the first embalming school.

Undertakers had experimented with other techniques to preserve the body before they finally embraced embalming. In the trade's early days, they would surround the body with ice to slow the putrefaction process. But it required constant attention and was of limited impact. By 1890 arterial embalming, the process by which embalming fluid was pumped into an artery while blood was drained out of a vein, had emerged as the superior process.

Embalming was seen as both sanitary and therapeutic. The sanitary benefit supposedly came from the protection it afforded the family and other mourners from infection from an otherwise germ-ridden corpse. Until 1910, when it was largely replaced by formaldehyde, arsenic was the main ingredient in North American embalming fluid. Arsenic was used because it was toxic, killing the microorganisms that led to decomposition. Out of concern for the health of embalmers, arsenic was banned in the early twentieth century. Since an embalmer might use between six ounces to three pounds of arsenic per person, a cemetery that buried a thousand embalmed people between 1880 and 1910 might contain a ton of arsenic. It has not gone away; tests have shown elevated arsenic levels in the groundwater near old cemeteries.[6]

The therapeutic role of the funeral, and of embalming, was to help people become reconciled to loss. With embalming came the use of makeup, and dressing and posing the corpse in ways that resembled a person at rest, albeit fully clothed. For many, the goal was to completely dispel the idea that the person was dead. Given that embalming rarely managed to leave such an impression, others suggested that the profession was helping people both say good-bye to the person they knew and to come to grips with the reality of their death. The restated goal was to capture both life and death — an image that would allow a memory but also emphasize that the person had died.

Initially undertakers usually did their work on what was termed a cooling board (as in blues singer Son House's "Death Letter Blues," in which the singer laments that "When I got there, she was laying on the cooling board"), either in the home of the deceased or the church in which the funeral was to take place. Well into the twentieth century it was still quite common for the funeral to take place in the home, usually in the parlour, the most highly furnished room in the house that was reserved for special occasions. Funeral directors, as undertakers increasingly styled themselves, stressed the continuity with this practice by calling their establishments funeral parlours. These were usually a strange mixture of place of business, chapel, morgue, surgery and residence — since the funeral director's family usually lived on the premises. The biography of Violet Guymer, Canada's first licensed female director, tells of how, behind her back, her children would play hide-and-seek in the viewing rooms, occasionally hiding in a closed but empty casket. Guymer herself held Halloween parties in the morgue, the highlight of which would be a game called John Brown's Body. In the dark, people passed around pieces of food and other items alleged to be portions of Mr. Brown's mouldering body — props included skinned grapes, a leg of ham and a blown-up rubber glove.[7]

Taking death out of the family parlour and moving it to the commercial funeral parlour was both a stroke of financial genius and necessity since fewer and fewer homes had parlours. It was not uncommon for the new funeral home to have a slumber room, similar to a bedroom, in which family members could visit with the corpse in the period before the funeral. While there was an effort not to make the funeral home too glum or sombre, most of the embellishments, through such touches as the purchase of a pipe organ, contributed to the sense of solemnity.[8]

DEATH IN CANADA

The rise of the funeral home coincided, not surprisingly, with tremendous changes in how death was dealt with in Canada. In the twentieth century, death moved from the home to the hospital, becoming much less likely to be the result of an epidemic and far more likely to be the result of a degenerative disease. This had not been the pattern in previous centuries.

While life expectancies for Aboriginal people at the time of first European contact were likely to be an average of thirty to forty years, about the same as they were in Europe, it was not unknown for Aboriginal people to live lengthy lives.[9] John Ballendeen, the Hudson's Bay Company's chief officer at York Factory on Hudson Bay wrote in 1800 of an Aboriginal woman who he estimated to "be upwards of one hundred years old. Her voice is still strong and speaks as well at present as I ever knew her."[10] Historian Renée Fossett writes that in times of a food crisis among the Inuit "elderly people were generally the first to offer to leave their bodies in order to enhance the survival chances of the rest of the community. Some of them deliberately placed their bodies in situations where death of the body would inevitably result, such as walking away from the village during blizzard or remaining on an ice flow about to be swept out to sea."[11]

For Aboriginal people, death was common and highly visible within the community. Throughout what was to become Canada, Aboriginal people developed a wide range of rites for treating and honouring the dead. Corpses might be cremated, mummified, buried under stones or wood, placed in trees or on a scaffold, sent down a river in a canoe or placed in an urn or ossuary.[12] In the summer of 1784 Questach, the captain of the Lowland Cree Goose Hunters at Albany Fort, died. According to Hudson's Bay Company official Edward Jarvis, he had been "declining ever since the famine he underwent in the winter." Following his death, his fellow hunters placed him in a "wooden tomb built in a very permanent manner." Jarvis wrote that Questach was buried with "more solemnity and ceremony than ever I saw on like occasion."[13]

European immigration brought with it a variety of infectious diseases for which Aboriginal people had no immunity. Thousands upon thousands died, while the weakened survivors fell prey to starvation. While they had greater immunity than Aboriginal people, the newcomers were not spared — infectious disease was to claim the life of at least one of every four Europeans who immigrated to Canada prior to 1891.[14]

In his discussion of childhood in New France, historian Peter Moogk bleakly concludes, "Death was no stranger to the people of New France. The population was ravaged by smallpox epidemics, by war, and, in the seaports, by shipborne infections. Nearly half of the adolescents in the colony had lost one parent."[15] Even today February and March are the deadliest months — in the nineteenth century, the risks were even greater. Maria Louisa Beleau was still a child when the harsh winter of 1816–17 carried her off. A witness at the inquest into this child's death said:

> The hovel in which the deceased had lived, with her mother, and two sisters, is not fit for a stable. It is open in many parts of the roof and on all sides. There is no other floor than the bare earth. It is a mere wooden stall; it has no window, nor any chimney. In the middle is a shallow hole made in the earth, in which there are marks of a fire having been made; and the smoke escaped through the open parts of the roof and sides. When I was there on Tuesday last, there was no fire in the hole.[16]

Women who did not die giving birth to their large families might die young, worn out by the exertions of raising so many children. Eliza Anne Chipman of the Annapolis Valley in Nova Scotia died at forty-six in 1853, having given birth to twelve children, four of whom died before her. As historian Margaret Conrad writes of this period, "cousins, siblings, relatives, and friends seemed to die off with unnerving regularity."[17] Alice Coalfleet of Hantsport, Nova Scotia, knew this only too well; in an eight-month period in 1892 a sister died in childbirth, another sister died at sea, her husband died in a separate marine disaster and her grandparents died.[18] Historian Bettina Bradbury writes that in nineteenth-century Montreal the children of the working class and the poorer French Canadians died in the greatest numbers, usually to intestinal disease and diarrhea. Only three of ever five infants born in Montreal in 1867, the year of Canadian Confederation, survived the year.[19]

In the nineteenth century people died at home, they died young and they died from accident or infectious disease such as tuberculosis. Up until the mid-twentieth century, hospitals were not seen as sites of healing or care, and, until the introduction of sterilization and germ theory, these views were justified. Public sewage systems, water purification, pasteurization and immunization, all the public-health innovations of the early twentieth century, had a dramatic impact on life expectancy. In the second half of the century the medical system became more effective at treating cancer and heart disease. In 1770 the death rate was 17 per thousand, by 1926 it was 13.5, by 1939 it was 10.4. By the end of the century it was under 7.[20] As fewer people died at home, it would become less common for people to organize the funeral in their own home.

A FAMILY BUSINESS

In Winnipeg in the early twentieth century, A.S. Bardal lacked the money to set up his own funeral chapel until he had the good luck to have his property expropriated by the Canadian Pacific Railway. In 1906 he used the money from the sale to build a large three-story building, complete with chapel, embalming room, offices and four apartments, right across the street from Winnipeg's General Hospital. For decades it was a true family business: A.S.'s sisters initially lived in apartments in the building, and his four sons went into the business, and as they married, many took apartments in the building. To this day it is still operated as a funeral home.

It was during the 1918–19 influenza epidemic that the Bardal home truly established itself in the community. The global epidemic killed 1200 people in Winnipeg. According Neil Bardal,

> My grandfather and the people working with him were absolutely exhausted. There was all this death and there was no one to pay for the funerals. The state would not help, so we got into barter situations. And my grandfather was very distressed because he was burying his friends. According to my aunt he considering leaving the trade, lamenting that, "All my friends are dying around me."

But he continued into the 1920s and prospered, due to the goodwill that the firm established during the epidemic. As the company grew, it provided what came to be known as the traditional funeral.

As the much fancier rectangular casket came to replace the traditional six-sided coffin, A.S. stopped building his own coffins. The creation of a continent-wide rail system had allowed for the emergence of large-scale manufacturers in a variety of commodities, including coffins. For example, while Bardal was able to buy most of his caskets from the Winnipeg Casket Company, he turned to a company in Three Rivers, Quebec, for high-end caskets. The Stein Manufacturing Company, which made caskets, produced a trade magazine, *The Casket*, through which it marketed ever more orna-mented caskets. The U.S. National Burial Case Association went so far as to fix a price for caskets.[21] Unlike coffins, caskets were meant to protect the corpse (the great unasked and unanswered question is, of course, from what does a dead body require protection). The 1912 Montross Sanitary Casket, for example, was advertised as indestructible, airtight and resistant to water, vermin and germs.[22]

PROFESSIONALIZING THE FUNERAL DIRECTOR

At the heart of all these developments was the newly emerging trade of funeral director. In 1882 the National Funeral Directors Association held its founding meeting in Rochester, New York. The newly formed association was quick to adopt a code that warned practitioners that "high-toned morality" was a professional imperative.[23] According to historian James Farrell,

> The required traits of the professional undertaker included mastery of self and situations, delicacy and tact, urbane manners, the ability to be all things to all people of all classes, quietness and quickness, and a temperament of assured equanimity. Well-dressed and well-groomed, ever alert to appearances, the professional undertaker was to be, in short, a gentleman.[24]

It was a trade beset by self-doubt. Were they tradesmen or professionals? Unlike most professions, there were no insuperable academic or training hurdles to overcome — in the early twentieth century, embalming schools offering six-week courses cropped up across the United States. By the 1930s the courses generally lasted for nine months. Did the funeral director control a body of specialized knowledge that allowed them to perform a unique service and therefore gave them the right to the perquisites of a profession, including the right to exclude others from the profession? Or was their personal character the essence of their craft and skill? The authors of the 1934 book *The Evolution of the American Funeral Director* made the claim, "Embalming in this country is now a recognized science, and Funeral Directing has attained the dignity of a profession."[25] The frequency with which this claim has been repeated through the trade's history is a sign of its continuing insecurity.

The funeral director was also assuming control over the funeral, giving "comfort to the bereaved family by handling the numerous details relative to a funeral which under the circumstances would prove distressing."[26] As the funeral directors took control of the funeral, they displaced both the clergy and the family. There was less and less place for use of the funeral as an object lesson that reminded assembled mourners of the yawning abyss that awaited them if they did not get right with God. *The Embalmer's Monthly* said the undertaker "should relieve the bereaved family of all responsibility of a burden they should, under no circumstances, carry in addition to the one already upon them."[27] In the process, the undertaker, whose role was that of chief mourner, became the funeral director who stage-managed a ceremony of consolation. According to Neil Bardal, his grandfather A.S. Bardal fit the bill completely: "When he would come into a place where a death took place, he announced 'Here is what I am going to do, here is what is going to happen.'"

In the early twentieth century most jurisdictions established boards of embalmers and funeral directors, which were given the responsibility of licensing embalmers. Embalming, however, was to remain the only aspect of the funeral director's work for which certification was required. The public never fully granted the undertaker the esteem given to other professions. Part of the problem was the practice of making the price of the casket the entire price of the funeral. This could be seen as an attempt to move the focus of the funeral away from death and towards the more mundane purchase of a commodity. Like any aspiring professionals, funeral directors tried to limit competition; as early as 1883 funeral directors were seeking to have suppliers restrict their sales to reputable undertakers. In the United States, the trade was dogged by the fact that too many people were harkening to its call. From 1880 to 1920 the number of undertakers doubled, while the number of deaths per undertaker fell from 194.2 to 56.6.[28] The one thing competition did not do was drive down the price of a funeral: over the same period that the number of undertakers doubled, the cost of a funeral rose by 250 percent.[29]

It is useful to think of the growth of the funeral industry as another example of what the American social theorist Immanuel Wallerstein refers to as the commodification of everything. By that he meant that the history of capitalism involves a process in which all the goods and services that were once produced by families and communities for their own consumption are eventually turned into commodities that are produced for profit. In the same way that many people no longer eat most of their meals at home, care for their own children or make their own soap, we no longer bury our dead. The funeral director is no more (or less) culpable for these developments than the owners of restaurants, child-care centres or detergent companies for turning meals, love and cleaning into commodities.[30]

The newly emergent industry was not without its critics. In his memoir *Life on the Mississippi*, the American novelist and social commentator Mark Twain described an encounter with an old friend who had gone into the undertaking business in New Orleans. Claiming that undertaking was the dead surest business in Christendom, his friend explained, "A rich man won't have anything but your very best; and you can just pile it on, too — pile it on and sock it to him — he won't ever holler. And you take a poor man, and if you work him right he'll bust himself on a single lay-out."[31] Twain went on to give an unflattering picture of the profession and the industry, concluding that it was his preference to be cremated. In 1928 the Metropolitan Life Insurance Company, concerned that its policy holders were being overcharged for funerals, published *Funeral Costs, What They Average; Are They Too High; Can They Be Reduced?* It concluded that prices were driven by a growing number of competitors and a decline in the death rate. Lamentably, competition did not drive down prices. The report's author John Gebhart wrote, "Competition among undertakers, to put it bluntly, is chiefly for the possession of bodies. Once the undertaker secures possession of the body, he can usually charge all that the traffic will bear."[32] Like many other critics of the funeral industry, there is a streak of elitism in Gebhart's work; he believed the poor were paying for funerals that were out of keeping with their station in life and squandering money on extravagant ceremonies. Good taste, in his view, was expressed in a simple and economic funeral.[33] The American way of death also came under attack from some religious leaders, who recognized the emphasis on the embalmed body represented a very unchristian focus on the body as opposed to the spirit. Indeed, the priest or minister was being reduced to a walk-on role in a process that focussed on loss and memory rather than the next and greatest step in the soul's journey. Which is not to say that on the whole funeral directors did not cultivate positive working relations with members of the clergy across North America.

A COMMUNITY-BASED BUSINESS

A.S. Bardal was a larger than life figure in the local Icelandic community and the local funeral profession. A devout Lutheran, he was active in the temperance movement and poured endless amounts of money into a local inventor's fruitless efforts to develop a carburetor intended to dramatically improve gasoline mileage. Proud of his Icelandic heritage, he funded a local school for Icelandic students and made numerous trips back to Iceland at a time when a Winnipegger had to take train to Montreal and sail to Scotland before they could catch a ship headed for Iceland. During these days the Icelandic community was deeply split between the Unitarians and Lutherans, but A.S., as the community funeral director, was one of the few people who could move easily in both groups. He did not keep his opinions to himself and once ended a theological dispute with a leading Unitarian by telling him, "I don't care what you say, I will be the last to throw dirt in your face." When the gentleman died, the family came to A.S. to arrange the funeral only to get a phone call from their lawyer, who had just read the will and discovered that it expressly prohibited any dealings with Bardal. Professionally, he helped establish the Western Canadian Association of Funeral Directors. As the business grew, he moved to suburban North Kildonan, where he was elected reeve. Like many immigrants, his life was tinged with tragedy: his first wife Vigdis died of what was then termed consumption — the two daughters to whom she gave birth also died young. His second wife Margret, also of Icelandic background, gave birth to fourteen children, three of whom died in infancy.

A.S. was not, however, a great businessman. According to Neil Bardal, "Of all the funeral homes that grew out of that time, we were the least successful." Aside from devoting too much of his time to community activities, A.S. paid little attention to costs and profit margins and varied the cost with the customer. This was what Neil Bardal refers to as the Robin Hood system, under which better-off clients were expected to subsidize the funerals of poorer community members. One of the problems with this method was the scarcity of well-heeled Icelanders and Lutherans. While the Icelandic community placed a heavy stress on education, and many second- and third-generation Icelanders went on to prominent careers in the professional and business worlds, the early immigrants were people of modest means. It was also a tightly knit community in which everyone knew how much everyone else had been charged for a funeral. In short, the company had a loyal clientele, but one that it could not expect to get rich servicing. The Great Depression put a tremendous squeeze on the business. Once more, many of the clients could not pay or could not pay in cash. The company had to get into debt, and almost all of its possessions were mortgaged. By the end of the decade A.S. had to sell his suburban home and move back to the downtown funeral home.

Until the 1960s the Winnipeg funeral industry consisted of a little more than half a dozen funeral homes each with their own market niche. As Neil Bardal describes the situation, "Our family catered to Icelander and Lutherans. Gardiner did the important people, Leatherdales and Thomson's did the mid-range United Church, Mordues did the Anglo-Saxon business — the university crowd went there, Desjardins and Coutu did the French and Barkers did the Catholics. Dave Zawidosky ran a North-End location serving Eastern Europeans for the Leatherdales." One could tell if a person had outgrown their social class by their choice of funeral home. Neil Bardal recalls once being at the beach at Lake Winnipeg with this father and Wilf Gardiner when the news came over the radio that a senator of Icelandic background had died. Gardiner excused himself, saying he had better be getting back to the city to begin to make preparations. Perplexed, Neil asked his father why their family's funeral home would not be getting the business. After all, the senator was Icelandic. "My dad's reply was that 'senators are important people, and important people go to Gardiners.'"

It was a family business, but not one that Neil Bardal's father Njall had been keen to go into. Complaining that the family was too hoity-toity, he moved to Chicago at age nineteen, where he trained as a railway engineer. But he eventually attended Worsham's Mortuary School in Chicago and re-joined the family business in 1933. With the Great Depression raging, Njall's brothers Karl and Gerald also came to work in the family business in the 1930s. When World War II broke out Njall, who had joined the Winnipeg Grenadiers in the 1935 when it was a militia unit, was posted overseas — first to Bermuda and Jamaica, and then, fatefully to Hong Kong. Following the fall of Hong Kong to the Japanese Imperial Army in 1941, he was held prisoner until the war's end. He did not see his son Neil, who was born in 1940, for the first time until he returned home. Brother Gerry joined the navy, while Paul joined the air force. Karl also wished to volunteer, but stayed home to help run the family business. Afterwards, Njall, Karl and Gerard all returned to the family business — Njall willingly, Karl with gritted teeth. They were joined by Paul Bardal, the son of A.S.'s brother Pall who had worked alongside A.S. until Pall's death in 1928.

GROWING UP IN A FUNERAL HOME

Neil Bardal grew up in the funeral home speaking Icelandic. As a child, most of the people he associated with were relatives or other people of Icelandic descent. On returning from his first day of public school, he informed the family that there were plenty of foreigners, meaning English-speaking students, at his school. Neil's parents' apartment was right over the funeral chapel and family life ceased during a funeral service. Family members could not walk, could not flush the toilet, and Neil — who was musical — could certainly not play the piano. "I used to sit by the window looking out," says Bardal, "when my grandfather appeared on the street in his big raccoon coat, marshalling the funeral procession, I knew the time was coming when we could move around. At the same time, I was fascinated by what I saw."

The business was tough on the family in other ways — one never knew when a call might come in. Indeed, the two words "the call" are among the most loaded in the industry. It refers to the telephone call requesting the firm's services. (Instead of referring to how many deaths they handle, most funeral directors usually speak of how many calls they handle each year.) When the call came in the middle of the night two of the brothers would get up, collect the body and embalm it before going back to bed. Weekends at the lake could be cancelled by the call, as could attendance at school plays or musical performances. Neil Bardal recalls confronting his father for failing to attend his performance at the Winnipeg Music Festival:

> He said, "There is no way I can explain this to you except to say you will probably have to explain it to one of your kids one day. It is not that anybody else in this whole world is more important than you, but somebody needed me more at that time and you will have to just take that." I resented that for a long time.

From his early days in school Neil realized that as the funeral director's son he was marked out as different. It also gave him some cachet with the neighbourhood children. Says Bardal, "I would invite friends over and then ask them if they wanted to see the morgue. When we got down there one my uncles would see us and start yelling 'What the hell do you think you are doing here?' and chase us back up the stairs." While Bardal has no memory of the first time he saw a dead body, he has a distinct recollection of discovering his limits. His uncle Gerry, who had picked up some barbering skills in the navy, used to cut the hair of all the sons and nephews, who would sit on the tables used for prepping the corpses while they got their trims. One day Neil went down to the basement for his hair cut and saw his uncle giving a corpse a trim with the barber scissors. "He just wiped off the scissors with some Kleenex and he said 'sit down.' I said, 'Not on your life,' and never went back there. That was the last haircut."

A.S. owned the company until two weeks before his death in 1952 when his sons finally convinced him to incorporate and sell it to them and their cousin Paul. They were to spend most of their careers putting the business back on a sound financial footing. An active member of the Liberal Party, Paul served as city councillor, deputy mayor and member of the provincial legislature. Because of his public profile and financial acumen he became company president. With his military background and involvement in church activities, Njall was the next most prominent member of the firm. Karl and Gerald did most of the embalming, with Paul and Njall only getting involved in the embalming if it was someone they knew. The youngest of Njall's brothers, Paul, had only a limited involvement in the company, selling his shares in the late 1950s. All five of them were licensed embalmers. They kept all work in the family; painting, fixing engines, shovelling the snow off the sidewalk or washing the cars, it was all done by brothers, cousins or nephews. They not only paid off the company's debts, but they began to reinvest in the facility that had been allowed to deteriorate during the 1930s and 1940s.

Seeing the toll that the business exerted on the family, Neil Bardal vowed to himself that he would die before going into it. On finishing high school, he attended Winnipeg's United College, which, in the late 1950s, was a hotbed of political enthusiasm and controversy, particularly when well-liked economics professor Harry Crowe was fired for political comments he had made in a private letter. In the wake of the controversy a number of the faculty resigned from the college. Caught up in the spirit of the time, nineteen-year-old Neil was considering going into the ministry, when his father, with whom he had never had a close relationship, asked him to consider giving the funeral business a try. Neil wavered, but in response to his father's demand for an answer then and there, he agreed only to be told that his father had already enrolled him in a mortuary school in Toronto and bought him a ticket on a plane leaving in two days. Though he resented the presumption, Bardal did not have the nerve to confront his father.

To his surprise, he enjoyed the schooling and the work and realized that if he became a funeral director there would be time to pursue other activities. Like his grandfather, he could have a career and be involved in politics, the church or community activities. He, however, saw his future in eastern Canada. Then, just after he graduated in 1962, came a phone call from his father announcing that he was ill and might not survive. Neil rushed back to

Winnipeg, dropped his bags off at home and told his mother he was off to see father at the hospital. The news dumbfounded her, since she knew her husband was alive, well and playing billiards at the Legion. This time Neil had the courage to confront his father with his lie — but the elder Bardal had no problem brazening him out, saying "Yeah, I lied to you. If I had not told you that, would you be here?" Like his father before him, Neil found himself being dragged back into the family business. It must have seemed like a secure field to be entering. Whenever there was a death in the family, people called the home that their family had always used. And they expected the funeral home to provide a traditional funeral — which included embalming and a viewing in a pricey casket. It was a good thing and it looked like it would last forever.

CHAPTER 2

FUNERALS WITHOUT FINS

IN 1963 JESSICA MITFORD, THE DAUGHTER of a decidedly odd family of minor English aristocrats, published *The American Way of Death*. Mitford had become interested in the subject through the work of her husband, U.S. labour lawyer Robert Treuhaft. On a number of occasions he had done estate work for union members and, according to Mitford,

> began to notice, to his great irritation, that whenever the bread-winner of a family died, the hard-fought-for union death benefit, intended for the widow, would mysteriously end up in the pocket of an undertaker: whether the benefit was $1,000, or $1,200, or $1,500, that would be the exact sum charged for the funeral.[1]

Treuhaft helped establish a funeral cooperative in Berkeley, California, where he and Mitford lived, and encouraged her to write a magazine article about the funeral industry. The result was a mixture of satire and muckraking that she expanded into a full-length book. Mitford mined the funeral industry publications for details of various marketing strategies, mocked the cloying and self-serving nature of the funeral industry's public pronouncements, drew attention to the fact that embalming was a curiously American practice and reminded readers that the cost of dying was going up at a faster rate than the cost of living.

In the foreword to *The America Way of Death*, Mitford commented,

> This would normally be the place to say (as critics of the American funeral trade invariably do), "I am not, of course, speaking of the vast majority of ethical undertakers." But the majority of ethical undertakers is precisely the subject of this book.[2]

According to her, the undertaking profession as a whole exploited the consumer in a "disastrously unequal battle."[3] For example, the funeral director had worked out a near-scientific method of displaying caskets with the goal of selling caskets in the upper price range. Mitford deliciously skewered W.M. Krieger's stair-step method (also called the third-unit rule), in which the funeral director starts out by showing a casket that he suspects is outside the client's price bracket. This is followed by a low-end casket, with the expectation that, as with Goldilocks, the final purchase will be the one in the middle. A system known as the rebound method worked on a similar principle.

She concluded the introduction to her book by noting that in recent years many Americans had abandoned fancy gas-guzzling automobiles for European-style compact cars. "Could it be," she asked, "that the same cycle is working itself out in the attitudes towards the final return of dust to dust, that the American public is becoming sickened by ever more ornate and costly funerals, and that a status symbol of the future may indeed be the simplest kind of 'funeral without fins'?"[4]

The American Way of Death was a bestseller in Canada and the United States. Taken unawares, the funeral industry adopted a series of responses. Many hoped that Mitford and the book would simply go away, others pointed to Mitford's Communist background and suggested if she did not like either the American way of life or death, she should set sail for the more congenial shores of either the United Kingdom or the Union of Soviet Socialist Republics. Others refused to back down in the face of criticism over cost and pomp. In one industry insider's words, "A good funeral should be so different from a cheap service, should be so obvious in quality, that the purchaser doesn't have to exhibit the funeral bill to prove that he selected something in keeping with his sense of pride."[5] The National Funeral Directors Association published 100,000 copies of *For the Living*, a book that it commissioned to tell its side of the story. There were many religious leaders who came to the defense of the American funeral, pointing to the religious and therapeutic benefits of funerals — which Mitford had not disputed — and stressing the value of viewing the embalmed body as the moment of truth at which all denials of death collapse.[6]

While he is critical of many of Mitford's conclusions, historian Gary Laderman concedes that "Mitford singlehandedly revolutionized many critical details of the American funeral industry. Her book, in fact, permanently changed the public face of death in America."[7] Laderman likely places too much weight on the impact of Mitford's book, but it is fair to say that from 1963 onward the percentage of cremations in the United States and Canada began to increase dramatically (as did immigration from south-east Asia, which increased the number of people for whom cremation was a key element of a traditional funeral).

CREMATION

Like embalming, cremation is a modern practice with a long lineage. With the notable exceptions of the Egyptians, Jews and Chinese, it was common throughout the ancient world. The sacred Hindu texts speak of cremation as a process that releases the soul. Cremation was also common in classical Greece and Rome. Ovid's poem *The Metamorphoses* gives a detailed depiction of the cremation of Hercules, the hero who was half man, half god. In Ovid's telling, fire consumed Hercules' human body while his divine spirit rose to heaven. While neither the Torah nor the New Testament take a stand on cremation, historian Stephen Prothero notes that the only people to be cremated in the Old Testament are abominable.[8] The Christian emphasis on belief in the resurrection of the body meant that early Christian leaders were not comfortable with cremation, but it was not until 789 that Charlemagne, the first Holy Roman Emperor, banned cremation.

Cremation remained a continuous practice in Asia. Devout Hindus seek to be incinerated in the city of Varansi and to have their ashes deposited in the Ganges River. The Buddha was cremated upon his death and cremation has remained common, although not required within the Buddhist tradition. Cremation did not kindle much interest among people of European backgrounds until the French revolutionaries, keen on developing new traditions, began promoting it. Like their attempt to rename the months of the year, this was a short-lived enthusiasm, and the real turn came in the 1870s when a number of European physicians, fearful that crowded burial grounds were the source of plague and pollution, came out in favour of cremation as a healthier and more civilized way to dispose of a human body. One of the most distinguished of these advocates was Queen Victoria's personal surgeon, Dr. Henry Thompson. He was writing at a time when medical professionals attributed the spread of plagues and diseases to miasma, air that was polluted by decaying matter. Burial grounds were seen as sites of decay and pollution, threatening air and water supplies. Cremation seemed a sensible public-health measure. But there was also an aesthetic argument in favour of cremation; its advocates saw it as much more beautiful and refined than the slow decay that follows earth burial. Finally, some pro-cremationists were simply afraid of being buried alive. Henry Laurens, who in 1792 became the first man of European ancestry to be cremated in North America, chose the option because his daughter, after being declared dead of smallpox, made a miraculous recovery shortly before she was to be buried.[9]

The modern cremation movement took root in North America in December 1876 in Washington, Pennsylvania, when Henry Steel Olcott and Dr. Francis Julian LeMoyne officiated over the cremation of Baron Joseph Henry Louis Charles De Palm. The leaders of the cremation movement, and it was a movement, were among the social purifiers of the late-nineteenth century, men and women who were roused into action in response to the social problems that they saw arising from industrialization, urbanization and immigration. Among their numbers in both the United States and Canada could be found prominent advocates of women's rights, free thinkers and liberal churchmen. While many of these people came from the comfortable middle classes, the pro-cremationists occupied positions on its fringes. LeMoyne, who built North America's first crematory on his own property in Washington, Pennsylvania, had been a principled opponent of slavery (he apparently helped runaway slaves escape to Canada) and of bathing (he was convinced that God had not intended the human body and water to come into contact). Olcott was a spiritualist, a co-founder of the Theosophical Society and, in his later years, a convert to Buddhism. An impoverished minor member of the Austrian aristocracy, De Palm was both fearful of being buried alive and an admirer of Eastern philosophies.[10]

Because there was a four-month delay between his death and his cremation, De Palm was embalmed and his ashes, after a short period of storage in the offices of the Theosophical Society, were later scattered over New York harbour. Despite, or perhaps because of the tremendous publicity that attended the cremation, the practice did not catch on. In the nineteenth century cremation remained a marginal movement. Crematories were expensive to build and maintain, and in numerous locations in the United States cremation societies raised money for years only to conclude that they would never have sufficient funds to build a crematory. Lemoyne's crematory was in operation for twenty-six years and was used less than twice a year. Fewer than 1 percent of deaths in the United States were followed by cremation in 1900; as late as 1963 this number was only 3.7 percent.

The strongest opposition came from the Roman Catholic Church, which in 1886 forbade Catholics from being cremated or joining cremation societies. Catholic leaders saw it as another example of Protestantism's failure to recognize the centrality of the concept of the resurrection of the body.[11] The cremation advocates challenged those who said that they were preventing the final resurrection by pointing out that if God could reconstitute decayed bodies, he would be able to work the same miracle on ashes.

Starting in the early twentieth century, cremation became more of a business and less of a cause as a number of privately run crematories were established in the United States, leading to the founding of the Cremation Association of America (now the Cremation Association of North America) in 1913. The crematory operators were still beset by numerous technical problems such as smoke and smell. By 1919 there were seventy crematories in the United States. Many of these were affiliated with cemeteries since the common practice was to bury the incinerated ashes. Not surprisingly, crematory operators were often opposed to the scattering of ashes and, to impede the practice, they would refuse to crush the remains. For example, the association urged its members not to crush or scatter, and as a result crematories that once permitted scattering on site later banned it. During this period, cremation, which had initially been a public event that people attended, became part of a private, behind-the-scenes process.[12]

Along with some church leaders, funeral directors remained the most vigourous opponents of cremation. Embalming, viewing and ever more ornate funeral caskets, the central elements in the undertaking business, all stressed the preservation of the body. To most funeral directors, cremation was a repudiation of their craft and a threat to their industry. Crematory operators were much more conciliatory, pointing out that cremation was not an alternative to embalming. It was after all quite possible to embalm the body, hold a viewing and then cremate both the body and the casket. Funeral directors, however, were having none of this. As Neil Bardal recalls,

> The old-line funeral director would give someone a blast if they asked for cremation. "What? Are you crazy? Get out of here. You want me to shovel on the coal to burn up your father. That's an indignity. That's an indignity, take your business elsewhere. Just go and do it without any sort of ceremony at all!" And a lot of people said, "Okay, that is just what we will do."

CREMATION IN CANADA

Members of Montreal's medical community were among the first Canadian advocates of cremation. Noted McGill University professors William Osler and George Baynes spoke of the health hazards of burial, and Baynes published the pamphlet *Disposal of the Dead: By Land, by Water, or by Fire* in 1875. In the 1880s some members of Montreal's Protestant community began pressuring the Mount Royal Cemetery to provide cremation services. In 1897 brewery heir John H.R. Molson, a convert to Unitarianism, left the cemetery $10,000 to build a crematory.[13] According to historian Brian Young, the cemetery's superintendent Ormiston Roy objected to the high costs of burial, the crassness of funeral directors and, particularly, their appropriation of authority over the cemetery site.[14] However, it was not until tobacco magnate Sir William Christopher Macdonald presented the cemetery with an offer to build a crematory at the cemetery with his own money that the project finally got off the ground. Young says that the iconoclastic Macdonald, with his industrialist's belief in technology and efficiency, effectively imposed cremation on the cemetery.

Even with Macdonald's money in hand, the cemetery had a number of obstacles to surmount, the prime one being the opposition of the Roman Catholic Church. To operate the crematory, the cemetery needed an amendment to its provincial charter. To placate the Catholic Church, the amended charter stated that the cemetery could cremate only Protestants who had specifically expressed a desire to be cremated (preferably in their will). Furthermore, the cemetery was prohibited from cremating anyone who died a violent death. The crematory was built next to a new chapel and conservatory, meaning that the service, cremation and interment could follow each other in one location. The cemetery also provided low-cost coffins with papier-mâché ornamentation. The kerosene furnaces reached a temperature of 1100°C, reducing a body to ash in two hours. The first modern cremation in Canada took place on April 18, 1902, when the body of Senator Alexander Walker was cremated at the Mount Royal Cemetery.

The Mount Royal Cemetery encouraged families to bury cremated remains in a rocky part of the cemetery that was not appropriate for normal burial or to place them in its columbarium (a structure with individual niches for urns containing cremated remains). While the initial Montreal proponents of cremation were medical men worried about the health aspects of cremation and millionaires who certainly did not need to worry about the cost of a funeral (Macdonald bequeathed $100,000 to the crematory in 1916), at a cost of ten dollars for a cremation in 1913, the Mount Royal crematory made a low-cost funeral possible.[15]

However, for Canadians cremation was to remain a distinctly minority taste for the first two-thirds of the twentieth century. The second Canadian crematory, the art deco Vancouver Crematorium, opened in 1912, while the first crematory in Ontario, for example, was not constructed until 1933, when one was built at the Toronto Necropolis cemetery. James S. Woodsworth, the first leader of the Co-operative Commonwealth Federation, a predecessor to the New Democratic Party, was an early adaptor. Cremated in 1942, his ashes were spread from a family boat over Vancouver's English Bay. Unfortunately the night before the scattering was scheduled to take place, his son Charles had a boating accident that left a hole in the cruiser. As a result, other family members dispersed the ashes while Charles and his friends were bailing away to keep the boat afloat.[16]

MEMORIAL SOCIETIES

In the mid-1930s funeral industry critics and cremationists came together in an important way. In 1937 the Reverend Fred Shorter of the Congregational Church of Seattle helped found the People's Memorial Association. Shorter was an advocate of direct cremation: no embalming, no viewing and no coffin. The association reached an agreement with a local funeral home to cremate members for fifty dollars each. By 1950 it had over 600 members, and its success spurred the creation of other memorial associations (usually referred to as memorial societies) across North America and the eventual formation of the Continental Association of Funeral and Memorial Societies in 1962. In his history of cremation in the United States, Stephen Prothero writes that these societies

> were forceful advocates for the dignity, propriety, and economy of cremation. All championed spiritual over material values, criticizing the traditional funeral as materialistic and praising cremation as

spiritual. Most were staffed entirely by volunteers, and many were led by Unitarians, Quakers, and other liberal Protestants.[17]

The tiny Unitarian movement formed the basis for the memorial society movement in Canada. Originally a liberal, freethinking Christian faith, Unitarianism by the 1950s was evolving into a largely humanist and spiritualist movement. Its members placed a heavy emphasis on personal responsibility and social action and were involved in many Canadian social movements. In 1954 Montreal Unitarian minister Angus Campbell preached a sermon that was critical of the traditional funeral, which he said was characterized by vulgarity and pseudo-religion. Shortly afterwards, congregation members set about establishing a local memorial society. From the outset the goal was to reach beyond the Unitarian movement, and the society had two non-Unitarians on its first board of directors. Slowly, memorial societies were established in cities across the country, usually with Unitarians providing the initiative. As in the United States, the societies negotiated agreements with local funeral companies to provide low-cost funerals to society members.[18]

In October 1956 founders of the Memorial Society of British Columbia sought to "promote dignity and simplicity in funeral rites; to arrange, in advance of death, for its members and their families such lawful disposition of their remains as they desire; and to arrange memorial services."[19] Despite such high-minded goals, the society found that no funeral director in the province was willing to deal with it. The society's futile search for a funeral director who would provide a service at a fixed price with no pressure on the customer to buy a more expensive package ended in 1961 when Doug Foreman, an unemployed ticket-taker on the Second Narrows Bridge in Vancouver, heard from some friends about the memorial society's problems.

Foreman bought a second-hand station wagon, rented warehouse space in Vancouver's north shore, put his carpentry skills to work making coffins and in 1961 went into business as First Memorial Services. The memorial society entered into an exclusive contract with him — but in the early years its members were disobligingly healthy. Foreman did seven funerals the first year and thirteen the next. Despite these low figures, the initial industry response to First Memorial was hostile; funeral homes threatened to boycott companies that sold him coffins, pressured a hearse service not to deal with him and advised a crematory not to do business with First Memorial. The funeral industry unsuccessfully lobbied the government to make changes to the regulatory process that would have put First Memorial out of business. The memorial society members themselves were very pleased with First Memorial. Unitarian minister Philip Hewett, one of the original founders of the Memorial Society of British Columbia, recalls, "The general benefit was no hassle, no haggle. People would know that they were doing what the deceased would have wanted and was congruent with that person's life."

Unlike most other memorial societies across Canada, the Memorial Society of British Columbia was able to reach beyond its traditional base, which Jessica Mitford once described as "Unitarians, Quakers, eggheads and old farts."[20] Society secretary Jean Mohart worked for the International Woodworkers of America, one of the largest and most dynamic unions of the period. Active in both the New Democratic Party and the cooperative movement, she used these connections to recruit members at a rapid pace. The society soon became the largest in the country, growing to 80,000 members by 1976.[21] When Foreman no longer had time to build his own coffins, he discovered that none of the Vancouver-area casket companies were prepared to sell to him. Eventually he found a small company in the British Columbia interior that was willing to deal with a company that the industry viewed as an adjunct of the memorial society. When Foreman sought to build his own crematory, the industry opposed him, saying the province already had too many crematories. And as the society grew it not only took in an ever-larger share of the funeral market, it forced all the other funeral homes in British Columbia to keep their prices down. Today the Memorial Society of British Columbia has over 200,000 members and is the largest memorial society in North America. However, First Memorial is no longer a family business. Doug Foreman died in the 1980s, and after running the business for nearly a decade his daughter and son-in-law sold the business to Service Corporation International, a U.S.-based funeral corporation in 1989.

CREMATION CATCHES FIRE

The year 1963 marked a turning point in the history of the North American funeral. It was not only the year of the publication of *The American Way of Death*, it was the year the Roman Catholic Church relaxed its ban on cremation. While cremated remains were still banned from funeral masses, and priests were still forbidden to accompany bodies to — or perform services at — crematories, it was no longer a sin to be cremated.

Starting on the West Coast of Canada and the United States, cremation began to catch on. The U.S. cremation rate jumped from 3.7 percent in 1963 to 4.5 percent in 1969, 9.4 percent in 1979, and hit 25 percent by the end of the century.[22] One of the most flamboyant cremation providers was the San Francisco Poseidon Society, which promised to scatter ashes from a yacht into San Francisco Bay. Funeral directors had begun to learn the lesson, propounded by the opportunistic aristocrat Tancredi in Giuseppe di Lampedusa's novel *The Leopard*, "for things to remain the same, everything must change." Michael Kubasak, a funeral director and the future vice-president of the giant funeral corporation SCI, wrote in his 1990 book *Cremation and the Funeral Director* that funeral directors had to realize that cremation was just one more way of preparing the body for disposition. Historian Gary Laderman notes that Kubasak urged funeral directors "not to run from the cremation option for fear it represents an economic threat, but to assist clients in shaping the details of the final disposition by pointing out the value of having a ceremonial, communal last look at the casketed, embalmed body before it goes up in flames."[23] Industry publications recommended funeral directors employ many of the marketing techniques once associated with casket sales (these were the same methods that had been mocked by Mitford) to sell urns and other memorials. One recommendation, for example, was to stock at least one $2000 urn to make mid-priced urns look like bargains.[24] By the 1990s there were over one hundred urns on the market, some selling for over $3500.[25] The American funeral might no longer be traditional — but it still had fins.

BRINGING THE FINLESS FUNERAL TO WINNIPEG

While Neil Bardal certainly did not realize it at the time, Jessica Mitford's *The American Way of Death*, the rise of cremation and the unostentatious philosophy that guided the memorial society movement were to shape his life from 1963 onwards. His first response to Mitford's writings was a disbelieving "Oh, come on!" He knew that his father and uncles were not heartless predators or charlatans — they were honourable people, doing the right thing. Said Bardal,

> But as I read I was aware that she had identified our weaknesses: the lack of choice, the funeral directors' control of the industry, the pricey-ness. I also noted the way that the industry responded: she was either a Communist or she would go away. But I was beginning to think we might have to do something. It was scary to realize that you were going to have to make changes when you do not know what those changes are.

He recognized that a mortuary school education included lessons in selling: whether to knock on a steel casket with your fist or your palm (the palm makes it sound more solid).

At the drop of a hat, Bardal can transform himself into an old-time casket salesman. Lowering his voice, he intones, "Your father was an important man in this community, an outstanding individual. Yes, I think that a coffin like this would be fitting for a man of your father's position." At this point, I half-believe he knew my father. Furthermore, I can picture the coffin that he is talking about. And I am relieved that he appreciates my dad and can match him to an appropriate coffin. Neil waits a beat or two and then says,

"But if it were my money, I would look at one of these," and he pulls me over to look at other, equally imaginary, but certainly more expensive coffins. How can I reject the opinion of this man who had such a good read on my father?

During the 1950s cremation was a fringe practice in Canada and all but unavailable in Winnipeg, where the first crematory was not built until 1965. However, there was a tradition of cremation among some of the physicians at the Winnipeg General Hospital. When one of the doctors who favoured cremation died, a hospital pathologist, Dr. Donald Penner, would make arrangements with the Bardal Funeral Home, located across the street from the hospital, to have the body shipped to a Minneapolis crematory. Neil Bardal never forgot the conversation that took place one day when Dr. Penner dropped by the office to pick up the returned cremated remains of one of his colleagues. Njall Bardal passed the package over and then said to Dr. Penner, "You know, I have a building, a limousine, two hearses, two removal cars and a staff of ten. If everyone does what you are doing here…." He stopped, leaving the question to hang in the air. Dr. Penner raised his eyebrows and said, "You really should think about that." Sixteen-year-old Neil Bardal took it all in, dumbfounded — he spent years thinking about the question that his father had raised.

A decade later, the minister of Neil Bardal's church brought in Elizabeth Kübler-Ross, a psychiatrist, to speak to a group of nurses. Kübler-Ross's then-controversial work into death and dying would lead to a revolution in the treatment of the terminally ill. Bardal was invited to attend the lecture and then have lunch with the minister and Kübler-Ross. Her first words to Bardal were, "I have no respect for you or any of your ilk, but you are young enough that perhaps, if we talk for a while, I can straighten you out." She then went on to ask whether funeral directors ever asked families what they want, or did they assume that they knew what families need to get through their time of distress. When Bardal insisted that funeral directors knew what people needed and provided it, Kübler-Ross told him that because people did not trust funeral directors, they rarely told them what they really wanted. It was not an easy message to accept, but it was one that Bardal began to dwell on.

Even while he was having these doubts, Bardal retained a position in the mainstream of the profession, often being called upon to defend the industry in debates with its critics. In these exchanges he often stressed the point that funeral directors were honest business people and decent individuals. Jean Mohart, the driving force behind the Memorial Society of British Columbia, once just glared at him and said, "You always hide behind that. But if I can take the casket away from you, you are dead in the water. You will die financially." All Bardal could think was that she was right, so right.

Through this process, Neil Bardal came to realize he wanted to put a personal stamp on the business and move it a new direction. He can vividly remember when customers began to challenge him on the old pricing system that was based solely on the coffin. "What if we don't want it?" he was asked, and he answered, "What do you mean you don't want it, everybody wants it, everybody is going to need it!" Looking back on his youthful self-assurance, he comments, "What is remarkable is that no one really did need it."

Bardal also developed a close friendship with Norman Naylor, a minister in the Unitarian Church and the guiding force behind the Manitoba memorial society, which campaigned for low-cost funerals — usually cremations. Bardal upset many in the local funeral trade when he invited Naylor to speak to a meeting of the provincial funeral directors society. "My colleagues had a hard time forgiving me for bringing the enemy into our sacred halls," Bardal said. The groundwork was being laid for a transformation that would see Bardal try to remake the family-funeral business.

In 1969 Njall Bardal and his cousin Paul Bardal, who had been in the funeral business almost all their lives, received an offer for their Winnipeg funeral home from a U.S.-based conglomerate. From their perspective, the price was right. Njall's son Neil, however, did not want to see the family business sold. He and David Pritchard, who worked at the Bardal Funeral Home as a funeral director, put together a proposal that matched the U.S. offer. To get that sort of money, Bardal recalls they took on a tremendous debt: "The bankers sat us down and told us that if we worked fulltime and gave them all the money we made, we would basically be able to pay off the interest." Bardal and Pritchard's offer was accepted and they took over the business. The partners were hungry for work and made a dramatic success of the company, rarely taking any time off for family or holidays. Says Bardal,

> Once we went to visit our wives, who were at Grand Beach, and someone from the office phoned the hotel at Grand Beach to try and get in touch with us. When asked if she would take a message out to us at the beach, the receptionist asked, "How will I recognize them?" The answer was simple: "They'll be the only two men on the beach in business suits."

Neil Bardal's ideas about the industry were changing as his father was dying. During his father's illness, he would often drive him to Grand Beach for the day. On one such drive Njall turned to his son and said, "You know, if you were smart, when I go, you would cremate me and make a big deal about what you were doing." But when the time came, Neil was convinced by others that not to send his father out with a big traditional funeral would be seen as a lack of respect to the person and the profession. And so, Njall Bardal had a traditional funeral.

STARTING OVER

In 1979, Neil Bardal invoked a buy-sell clause in his partnership agreement with Pritchard, which he thought would lead to his buying out his partner. Instead, on October 5, 1979, Pritchard responded with an offer that forced Bardal out of what had been the family business and his childhood home. Bardal left the building that day and never returned. "I was thirty-nine and I realized that it would take me another twenty years to get back to the economic situation I was at then. But I had an idea of where I wanted to take this business and I wanted it to be much simpler. Which was good, because I went from a lucrative salary to making just $18,000 a year. But I have never been more happy than on this journey."

One of the first steps he took on this journey was to ask Unitarian minister Norman Naylor, "If you were given a blank piece of paper and asked to design a funeral business, what would you put on it?" He and Naylor talked extensively and travelled together to California, visiting companies that were on the leading edge of providing alternate funeral services, including the Neptune Society and its goateed owner, who liked to refer to himself as Colonel Cinders. One of the key lessons that Bardal learned from Naylor was the close relationship between dignity and simplicity. Naylor advised Bardal not to set up a facility that looked like a funeral home. Instead they created a bright establishment with the look of a suburban living room, reminiscent of the parlour that had been the site of the funeral in the days prior to the development of the funeral home.

Bardal was determined not have his economic success tied to the sale of products, particularly caskets and urns. "I think that the casket people took over this business," says Bardal. "The casket demanded the hearse and so on. Everything that we as undertakers did with the body was predicated on the product. I resented that because when you are appreciating the casket you are not even thinking about the body." Today, Bardal says, "I think caskets are passé and so is the attempt to equate the quality of the casket to the quality of the person." Bardal also has little time for the funeral home practice of selling special clothing for viewing and visitation. "Everyone," he snorts, "has clothes. Bring some from home so the body will look like the person you know."

He has not rejected all the components of the traditional funeral. For example, he remains a believer in the importance of the final visit with the body and the need for embalming to make sure that nothing goes awry at such an encounter. Bardal says,

> I tell them that if they wish, we can arrange a viewing. The person who is arranging the funeral might say, "No, I do not want to come to a viewing, but a cousin might." And if one comes, twenty will

come. There is no way that you can guarantee people will not touch the corpse. And if you are going to have people handling the corpse, it has to be embalmed.

Instead of focussing on the sale of product, Bardal wanted to stick as closely as possible to what he saw as the funeral director's mandate: the care of the body. It also meant that he had to be able to run a profitable business without counting on the support that came from the sale of caskets, which could often be marked up by more than 100 percent. He and Naylor wanted to design a business that could make a profit providing the most basic of services: what is known as "direct cremation, no service." "We would pick up the body, cremate it, and give back the remains without there being any funeral service or memorial service," says Bardal. In this he was responding to the message that he heard Dr. Penner deliver to his father and the warning that Jean Mohart had bluntly given him. There was a downside to eliminating product. "It is a lot easier to say that casket is worth seven hundred dollars than to determine the worth of the time of the people who are putting the funeral together plus the cost of transportation," he says.

Bardal realized that one of the reasons funerals were so expensive were the capital costs of goods that were used only for a relatively brief period. "In the old days," he recalls, "we built something for everything. There was a viewing room, a chapel, a reception area, a fleet of cars. It was grossly inefficient." Together with Naylor, Bardal planned a storefront operation that was located in a strip mall on Portage Avenue in Winnipeg. There was single meeting room that could be used for viewings, services and receptions. (At the end of the service people would file through the kitchen to pick up a cup of coffee and a sandwich. They would re-emerge into the room that had been used for the service to discover that the staff had re-arranged the chairs so the room could be used for the reception.) For larger services he would rent churches or community halls — places where people often felt more comfortable than a faux-solemn funeral home. Getting a municipal license to run a storefront funeral home was not easy. Bardal said he was opposed by both the funeral industry and city council. Finally, the city granted him a six-month probationary licence.

Initially Bardal offloaded the embalming and cremation, transporting the bodies to the crematories and embalmers in his own van rather than a hearse. Because he was not doing his own embalming or cremating, he called the firm Neil Bardal Inc., Family Funeral Counsellors. City of Winnipeg health inspectors were regularly in and out of his business during the early years, hoping to catch him doing some illegal embalming. It took three years before the city finally allowed him to do embalming at the funeral home itself.

Bardal says that Naylor also goaded him into heavily marketing his new business in ways then unheard of for the staid funeral industry. He put ads on buses and the radio and was regularly in the media during the company's early years. The message got out — there was a new sort of funeral director in town, he operated out of a storefront, he would do what you wanted and he was cheap. Because he did not stress casket sales, he had to abandon the traditional approach of having one price for a funeral — the price of the casket. "We decided to start with a blank piece of paper and price all of the parts," says Bardal. He did not post a price list, however, because he believed people would use a posted price list to plan their funeral rather than working through of a vision of what they wanted, getting a price and then working with him to see what needed to be done to make sure the family could afford the funeral.

By 1980 he was convinced that the future of the entire industry lay in cremation. "It always stuck in the back of my head that if people really thought about it, cremation would make sense," he says. But he was not going to adapt by developing new high-cost cremation-related products to sell his customers. Instead he wanted to bring them into the whole process. "Nobody would let us take the body out to the cemetery and bury it without them being there," says Bardal. "And I do not think that they should let us cremate the body unless they are there. The key is for the family to take ownership. Cremation allows you to do that better than the other system. In the old days, funeral directors and crematory operators did not want customers to know too much about what is going in the backroom. That was dumb, that was really dumb." So now, along with giving people a tour of his facility, he suggests that people come to the funeral home to view the embalming and be present for the cremation. Some people will actually turn on the retort and help sort the ashes. Most, however, are content to sit and read a magazine while the body is cremated. As Bardal notes, "At times like this, you really have nowhere else you have to be."

He and Naylor also experimented with ways to bring the cost of cremation down. Where some corporate funeral homes sought to make money out of cremation by insisting that clients use $750 cremation caskets, Bardal and Naylor pioneered the local use of the stiff cardboard cremation casket. Instead of charging upwards of a thousand-dollar rental fee for a casket that was used only for a viewing, Bardal developed a stiff-bodied shroud that could be placed over the cardboard casket.

While the funeral corporations have sought to turn memorialization into a profit centre, selling urns for several thousand dollars along with pricey niches in columbariums in which the urn and family mementoes can be stored, Bardal has established a simple scattering garden. He digs the trench in the garden, scatters the ashes and spreads mulch on top.

All of these changes were secondary, however, to what Bardal saw as his own change in approach to the profession. "For the first time," he says, "I was saying seriously to people 'I am the undertaker, I can do a lot of things. What would you like me to do? How do you see this, can you talk about and respond to that?' rather than saying 'Here is what we need to do.'" Bardal wanted to break with the tradition that held that the undertaker was the person who knew what had to be done and would take care of everything. He also asked himself what he would do when a member of his own family died. He describes his plan this way:

> The first thing I would want to know is where the body was. And then I would go there. Then I would bring the body to the funeral home and gather the family here. We would sit with the body. I would put the body into a coffin and put a shroud over it, and [we would] spend time together. When we have said our goodbyes, we would commit the body to the flames. It would be our choice to scatter the remains here in our scattering ground. The body is safest when you have returned it to the earth and there is no way to protect it from returning to the earth. Then we would go to the church and have a service and celebrate the life.

He realizes this is not what everyone would want. But by realizing that there is something specific that he would like helped him recognize that the funeral director's role is to assist others in discovering what it is that they want. Bardal says, "When we started to ask people seriously what they wanted, my life and my career changed dramatically."

Bardal had no trouble attracting customers, and each year was better than the one before. But to remain solvent he still had to keep dipping into the money he had received for the family business. Eventually his accountant convinced him that his former colleagues were right: in the long run they would not have to worry about him, because his fees were so low he would eventually go out of business. Not that his competitors were content to wait to let nature run his course. One day Bardal called the hearse rental company he had been dealing with to make arrangements for a particularly busy day only to be told that the company would no longer rent to him. When he asked why, he was told that the larger firms had made it clear that if he continued to rent to Bardal he would lose their business. It was too big a risk for him to take. "I called all sorts of people who I thought were my friends, but I could not rent a hearse to save my life," he says. He eventually tracked down a dealership with a hearse, only to be told that he could not rent the vehicle. In the end, he bought "a very cheap hearse for a very big price." At the same time, the companies with whom he was contracting out the embalming and cremation work were starting to raise their prices.

In response to these pressures, in 1982 Bardal purchased a crematory across the street from Winnipeg's Brookside Cemetery. It is as out of the way as his office on Portage Avenue is accessible. But it has become the company headquarters, the place where the embalming, cremating and viewing can be carried out. When Bardal purchased his crematory, he inherited the cremated remains of over 400 people that had never been claimed. He set about tracking down the families and returning the remains. In the end he was left with the remains of over fifty people. After taking all the steps required by law, he spread their ashes in the scattering garden he established outside the crematory.

Some lessons were learned the hard way. For example, when ashes are to be scattered, it is important that everyone present know exactly what is about to happen. When Bardal, in accordance with the wishes of the deceased, scattered a United Church minister's remains into an open grave at the Kildonan cemetery, the minister's sister keeled over in a faint. Nor were every one of his innovations successful. At a time when all the other funeral directors drove the minister to the cemetery in a Cadillac as the lead car in a funeral, he bought a small Volkswagen Rabbit. Not even Norman Naylor approved of this: with his tongue in his cheek as he folded himself into the tiny car, Naylor admonished Bardal, "I never told you to do this." An Anglican minister with an even more elevated view of his position in the community simply refused to get in the car. Nor were family members happy to discover that he had replaced the traditional hearse with a van. On more than one occasion, he recalls a disappointed customer asking, "Don't you have a hearse? I thought my father would ride in a hearse." These days the company fleet once more includes a hearse.

Today, Bardal and Sons is not the cheapest funeral parlour in Winnipeg. Indeed its success has spawned imitators who have set up various storefront operations throughout the city, one in a former fish-and-chip franchise shop. Bardal figures that, for the most part, they will have to bring their prices up once they realize that their revenues are not meeting all their costs. While he is constantly monitoring his costs, he also believes he continues to push into new frontiers and annoy his colleagues. Currently, his scattering garden is just outside his crematory, which means that it cannot be used during the long Manitoba winters. As a result, he plans to build an atrium over the garden and incorporate it into the crematory. The large funeral corporations opposed the expansion, claiming that Bardal was going into the cemetery business and ought to be so regulated. He took them on, noting that the corporate cemetery owners would not be satisfied until everyone was obliged to dispose of their cremated remains in a cemetery.

He remains fascinated by the challenges of what has come to be termed green burial: a form of earth burial that is simple, yet remains reverential. He feels it is best to inter the body without a coffin — wrapped in some form of winding sheet. But, he says, some members of the family will want to be there, and wonders what their sensibilities will demand. Should the body be placed on a board? How do you lower it down gently? What sort of lift would be appropriate in a green burial? "Screws, nails, even the casket — they don't belong in the ground — only the body belongs there," he adds. It might be possible to make use of the cardboard boxes currently used for cremations, but then again, he notes the plain pine box has a certain cultural resonance.

It is worthwhile to recall that Neil Bardal is not unique, even in Winnipeg. In many centres across Canada, there have been family- funeral directors who have sought to carve out an innovative response to the changes that began to wash over the industry in the 1960s. For example, in the late 1980s a Toronto funeral director started up what he called Direct Cremation and Burial Services, which provided low-cost cremation services. The funeral industry fought back and had the company, which by then was known as The Simple Alternative, declared a transfer service, which meant that it could not provide a full range of services to customers. The Simple Alternative, which was by then being operated by the non-profit Toronto Trust Cemeteries, transformed itself into a licensed funeral establishment that now offers wider range of alternative and traditional funeral services, all on a non-profit basis.[26] All of these alternative providers are being challenged by the rise of the multinational funeral corporations that will be described in Chapter 4. Before turning their history, the evolution of the North American cemetery must be sketched out.

CHAPTER 3

FROM THE FAMILY BURIAL GROUND TO THE MEMORIAL GARDEN

To THE LAYPERSON, THE WORD *FUNERAL* IS likely to imply all of the events that are set in train by a human death: a service (either religious or secular) and the disposal of the body — most commonly these days by either cremation or earth burial. The purchase of a lot in a cemetery and the interment of a body in that lot are, in many people's minds, all a part of either funeral planning or a funeral. However, for much of the last hundred years there has been a distinction between funeral services and their providers (the funeral directors and religious officials, who between them embalm, cremate, supply caskets, organize services and receptions, and handle the paperwork created by a death) and the cemetery services and their providers (selling cemetery lots, interring the body or the ashes, and selling and installing graveyard memorials). And until relatively recently, the history of cemeteries and funeral directors have followed separate courses.

While there is nothing new about burying the dead, cemeteries as we now know them — fields of stone in which people inter their loved ones in containers they expect to last forever — are relatively recent developments. Through much of human history people who buried their dead might chose to do so on a portion of farmland set aside for such uses. When Christian religions developed a belief that the bodies of believers should be buried in consecrated ground, it was not uncommon for a priest or minister to consecrate the family burial ground, allowing the family to continue with the practice of burying family members close to home. In pre-industrial Europe and North America, the grounds surrounding a parish church also served as graveyards, while those who died in poverty were often buried in unmarked fields. These paupers' burial grounds are usually called potters' fields, a name drawn from the Book of Matthew, which tells how Judas turned over the thirty pieces of silver he received for betraying Christ to the chief priests of Jerusalem. Viewing it as blood money, they chose not to put it in their treasury and instead used it to buy a potters' field (a field from which potters drew their clay) in which to bury strangers.

Nor did people expect to rest in peace forever. In the Middle Ages in Europe the churchyard would be bounded by charnel houses in whose upper floors would be found, artfully arranged, the skulls and limbs of those who had, for space reasons, been removed from tombs and graves.[1] The increased urbanization of the eighteenth and nineteenth century gave rise to the urban burial ground. In his book on the lives of the English working class, Friedrich Engels painted this chilling picture of one such field:

> The pauper burial-ground of St. Brides, London, is a bare morass, in use as a cemetery since the time of Charles II, and filled with heaps of bones; every Wednesday the paupers are thrown into a ditch fourteen feet deep; a curate rattles through the Litany at the top of his speed; the ditch is loosely covered in, to be reopened the next Wednesday, and filled with corpses as long as one more can be forced in. The putrefaction thus engendered contaminates the whole neighbourhood. In Manchester, the pauper burial-ground lies opposite to the Old Town, along the Irk; this, too, is a rough, desolate place. About two years ago a railroad was carried through it. If it had been a respectable cemetery, how the bourgeoisie and the clergy would have shrieked over the desecration! But it was a pauper burial-ground, the resting-place of the outcast and super-fluous, so no one concerned himself about the matter. It was not even thought worth while to convey the partially decayed bodies to the other side of the cemetery; they were heaped up just as it hap-pened, and piles were driven into newly made graves, so that the water oozed out of the swampy ground, pregnant with putrefying matter, and filled the neighbourhood with the most revolting and injurious gases. The disgusting brutality which accompanied this work I cannot describe in further detail.[2]

Nineteenth century Montreal had both Protestant and Roman Catholic burial grounds. Historian Brian Young notes that in times of epidemic these resources could be overwhelmed. In 1832 cholera killed 1950 people in Montreal, while in 1847 typhoid killed 3862 — and these are just the two most deadly epidemic years. In the 1832 plague, pits were dug to accom-modate all the victims of what one young medical student described as a "death carnival."[3] Young cites Alfred Perry, a young immigrant to the city who recalled a man coming to his family's house and taking away his father, over his mother's objections that he was not dead. Indeed, Mr. Perry revived just as he was about to be flung into the pit for the immigrant dead. He did not however survive the trip back home. To get the carter to take her husband to the English burial ground she had to promise him the suit of clothes off the dead man's back.[4] According to Young, these burial grounds were focussed on the "quick disposal of bodies. Nothing about their design or care pointed to any union of nature and death. That was to come with the rural cemetery movement."

THE RURAL CEMETERY

By the early nineteenth century there were growing concerns that urban burial grounds were sources of disease and illness. Although scientists had yet to develop germ theory, they believed rotting and putrefying bodies constituted a health hazard. Many church leaders were also concerned that the lower classes were using burial grounds as places of entertainment and amusement. Given that most cities had not invested in public parks, this was not surprising. The response, in both Europe and North America, was the rural cemetery movement. Since most of the rural cemeteries built in the ensuing years are now surrounded by urban development, the name might seem surprising to a contemporary reader. But when Père Lachaise Cemetery was built in 1804 it lay on the outskirts of Paris, just as Mount Auburn was several miles from Boston in 1831. Mount Hermon Cemetery was on the edge of Quebec City in 1848 when it became Canada's first rural cemetery.[5]

The rural cemetery, which took its name from *koimeterion*, the Greek word for sleeping chamber, grew up alongside the profession of landscape architecture. As a result, the new rural cemeteries were graced with trees, gentle hills, ponds, paths and curving winding avenues. They were designed as places to commune with God, nature and friends.[6] The cemetery was to edify, to take the terror away from death and make it familiar. And unlike the old burial ground or graveyard, they were to be cheerful places intended to sooth the sorrowful. It was also believed that properly designed and maintained rural cemeteries would provide moral and spiritual education to the slightly threatening and uncouth industrial workforce that was pooling in European and North American cities. In the 1843 *Layout and Management of Cemeteries*, John Claudius Loudon spoke of cemeteries as places "of instruction in architecture, sculpture, landscape gardening, arboriculture, botany, and in those important parts of general gardening, neatness order and high keeping."[7]

While initially all one needed to go into business as an undertaker was a wagon and some carpentry skills, it required a significant investment to establish a cemetery. Nor was it clear that they would be able to turn a profit. As a result, cemeteries were often municipal initiatives, or established by private corporations affiliated in some way with religious communities.

A CASE STUDY: THE MOUNT ROYAL CEMETERY

One of the largest and most striking rural cemeteries in Canada is the Mount Royal Cemetery in Montreal. Responding to both the overcrowding of the existing Montreal Protestant Burial Ground and the rural cemetery movement, a group of leading Protestant citizens along with one representative of the local Jewish community chartered the Mont Royal Cemetery in 1847. The board had representatives of the professions, banks, trade, industry, the world of politics and various benevolent societies.[8] John Samuel McCord, one of the founders of Mount Royal was active in the Natural History Society and the Horticultural Society — a sign of both the position that the cemetery founders held in society and the sources of their vision for the cemetery. The founders were looking for a location outside the city that would be able to serve them for at least a century. In the end they selected a farm on the northeast side of Mount Royal. A leader in the American cemetery landscaping movement produced a design that included carriage drives, vaults, a manmade lake, a house for the superintendent and imposing gates.

Certain portions of the cemetery were consecrated to each participating Protestant denomination as well as the Jewish faith. All who bought a plot had to declare their faith. Williams Squire, a Methodist minister and cholera victim, was the first person buried there in October 1852. That same year, the directors hired gardener Richard Sprigings as a live-in cemetery superintendent. This was becoming a trade that was passed on through the family; Sprigings, for example, employed two of his brothers, one of whom also lived at the cemetery. Historian Brian Young notes that just as the cemetery founders were the owners of the city's large industrial and financial concerns, many of its early employees were gardeners who had learned their trade while working on the grounds of the large estates that the founders lived in at the foot of Mount Royal. In the same way that furniture making and cartage served as an entry point to the undertaking trade, gardening served as an entrée to the cemetery profession.

The cemetery was subdivided into neighbourhoods, and as in every real estate market, the three key factors were location, location, location. A purchaser wanted the right view, access to transportation and to be surrounded by the right people. The gravesite should also reflect the purchaser's social standing — he might have the person who designed his mansion design his monument. Section A, once the highest point on Mount Royal, was where the elite were buried. It was not unusual, as new more prestigious sections were developed, for people to sell their plots and move up. Your headstone spoke of who you were in society, and it might do this at length. In the case of men, the emphasis was on profession and community involvement, for women it was piety and family. Nor did the rich have to be placed in the cold ground — they could have mausoleums, in effect, above-ground tombs. These might be free standing or cut into the mountain. In the nineteenth century they might cost as much as $5000. Brick mausoleums were required to have walls that were at least sixteen inches thick, stone walls had to be twenty-four inches thick, while coffins in mausoleums were to be encased it least four inches of cement.[9]

Young cites the McCord grave where Thomas McCord is buried with Peter McGill as his neighbour, Francis Hincks of the Grand Trunk and

Bishop Fulford all surrounding him. Pointing through his office window at McGill University, he notes that McCord had in death perfectly replicated the Golden Square Mile of Montreal where lived that very elite, with their churches and homes, and from where they directed the university and the cemetery.

While the rich were buried in family plots, the more humble, who, of course, always make up the numbers in a cemetery, were buried in sections that featured single graves. To some, burial mounds were unsightly, but to the poor, who could not afford a headstone, it was the only way to locate a burial spot. Where opponents of the mounds failed to have them eliminated, they usually managed to put on a limit on their size.

The directors made sure the cemetery bought land around the cemetery so that they could control its development. Canadian cemeteries also had to take into account the impact of climate. During the winter, the ground was too frozen for grave digging — instead, bodies were stored in a large receiving vault, which was locked to frustrate grave robbers and built into the side of a hill.[10] It was not until the twentieth century that advances in technology made it possible to dig graves year round.

Also within Mount Royal Cemetery, there was a free ground for those who could not afford to pay. Those who were buried in the free ground were buried anonymously: there was to be no marker and the gravesite would only be tended for five years. Young says that while it was important to the people who ran the cemetery that the poor be buried with dignity, "it was also important not to give those people recognition. Death meant that you were anonymous if you were poor." This anonymity was enforced by restrictions on the sorts of markers that could be used. The various Protestant denominations were supposed to pay for the member of their faith who had been buried in the free ground, but, according to the cemetery's director, by 1891 the cemetery had buried over 4000 bodies free of charge.[11] Aside from the various Protestant denominations, lots in the cemetery were also assigned to various ethnic and benevolent groups such as the Montreal Sailors' Institute, the Protestant Orphan's Asylum and the Chinese Colony of Quebec. Following the World War I, like many cemeteries in Canada, the Mount Royal Cemetery established a separate military section.

LAWN CEMETERIES

The rural cemetery has in large measure been replaced by the lawn cemetery, which is characterized by open fields, rolling hills and lawns rather than paths and can be seen as an aesthetic and financial reaction to the rural cemetery. In many cases, the rural cemetery had been a gated community in which different families had fenced in sections in which they built mausoleums, raised memorials and planted headstones. It was often the family's responsibility to maintain their plot. The result was often stark, gothic and prone to decay as iron fences rusted, stone walls collapsed and headstones were tipped on their sides. Cemeteries began to assume the cost of maintenance for cemeteries by establishing perpetual care funds (trust funds into which one paid when buying the cemetery lot). At the same time, cemetery directors became attracted to the lawn design, which was not only, in their opinion, cheerier and more attractive, but far cheaper to maintain.

The lawn cemetery showed the influence of the gardeners who had become cemetery managers. The key problem that they faced was how to provide perpetual care at a reasonable cost. The answer was the lawn. The lawn cemetery movement also reflected the dramatic social changes of the early twentieth century. Young refers to it as the democratization of the cemetery:

> These huge differences between paupers sections and the elite became more problematic as we moved into an egalitarian century. World War I really showed that we are living in a very dangerous century. We cannot put a John Molson up there on the mountain above the rest of us — his death really isn't a million times more important than some soldier who has gone off and been gassed and made the supreme sacrifice. So the lawn cemetery served a variety of purposes.

As opposed to being rural, lawn cemeteries were often built in suburbs, placing them much closer to where people lived.

When the Mount Royal Cemetery Company opened a second cemetery, known as Hawthorn-Dale, in east Montreal in 1910, it proclaimed a set of strict rules that made it clear that the cemetery directors were in charge and that the cemetery was being run on the lawn plan. The cemetery superintendent had final say as to what plants could be planted, while any fencing, seats and vases all needed his approval. Enclosures and mausoleums were banned and any items that exhibited rust were removed. Mounds were allowed only on the more expensive graves, and even then were limited in height.[12] The cemetery's long-time supervisor, Ormiston Roy, said that cemeteries "should be, as the name implies, sleeping places — places of rest and freedom from intrusion." In such places, "spreading lawns give a cheerful warmth and sunlight" and "branching trees give grateful shade, furnish pleasing objects to look at, and places for the birds to come each year and sing again their welcome songs."[13]

The cemetery business changed with the development of new technologies in the twentieth century. Backhoes, trucks and tractors transformed how work was done, and cars led to suburban development, which enveloped rural cemeteries. Where once it took three hours to dig a grave (and longer in bad weather), a backhoe got the work done in twenty minutes. Cemetery workers unionized, and in 1966 the Mount Royal workers went on strike for two weeks for a pay raise. A decade later they took to the picket lines once more to gain the five-day week.

There has been one other important change over time — people are far less likely to visit cemeteries than they have in the past. While family and friends may make a number of visits to the grave side in the first three months after the burial, the average North American grave receives only two visits from then on.[14] We may fear death, but apparently we no longer fear our dead ancestors or feel any compulsion to propitiate them. Most people visiting cemeteries are doing genealogical research, not visiting the dear departed.

THE MODERN CEMETERY INDUSTRY

For the first years of the twentieth century, cemetery services were provided by a wide range of religious, ethnic and fraternal organizations, municipal governments and other not-for-profit organizations. Even then, entrepreneurs were trying to get a share of the cemetery market. In 1913 local entrepreneurs offered Mount Royal Cemetery director Ormiston Roy $40,000 in stock to let them build a 900-body mausoleum at the cemetery. Roy rejected the bribe and the mausoleum. He viewed the community mausoleums as simply "filing cabinets for the dead," saw their promoters as "outside racketeers" and fended off their overtures well into the 1930s.[15]

The big change in the cemetery world came in the years after World War II with the rise of the private lawn cemetery corporations that adopted high-powered sales techniques to pre-sell cemetery plots. According to Young, these companies "marketed a familiar suburban environment, handy access from highways, carefree maintenance, and one-stop visitation, chapel, and burial space."[16] In 1947 the predecessor to Arbor Memorial Services (the second largest funeral and cemetery corporation in Canada) began developing what has grown into a network of forty-one private lawn cemeteries across Canada. Arbor became one of the first funeral "combinations" in 1983 when it opened a funeral home on its Winnipeg Chapel Lawn Cemetery property.[17] In 2006 it had thirteen funeral homes on cemetery properties. Its main competition comes from the Service Corporation International, which has nine cemeteries across the country (five of which have funeral homes located on the property). As far back as 1992 (the last year for which the federal government has published studies on the subject) the four largest cemetery firms in Canada accounted for 51 percent of the industry's revenue.[18]

Mount Royal Cemetery responded to these changes by going into the funeral business. It had a toehold in this side of the industry through its crematory, but in the 1970s it began to offer a much broader range of services.

It has since bought a funeral home and developed a large funeral complex on the mountain. In addition, it has sought to bring people into the cemetery by marketing itself as a heritage institution (by among other things, commissioning Young to write its history) and encouraging people to come to the cemetery on hiking and bird-watching expeditions, something that would have likely horrified the cemetery founders.

The corporate concentration of the funeral industry has taken place at same time that ethnic and fraternal organizations and municipal governments have stopped developing new cemeteries and most religious organizations have found themselves without the resources to buy new facilities. Given the expense of acquiring sufficient amounts of land and the complex zoning regulations that have to be adhered to, the corporate funeral homes appear confident that the future belongs to them.

CHAPTER 4

BIG DEATH COMES TO TOWN

CRITICISM OF THE UNDERTAKING TRADE seems to have commenced shortly after the first funeral director opened for business. In the face of allegations of overpricing, the undertaker's traditional argument was that his was a local, family-owned business. Though people might think that undertakers as a whole might be shady, they also tend to believe that the undertakers who had served their family — and often indeed their community — for decades were probably all right. If casket prices might be a bit high and options narrow to non-existent, still the funeral director seemed to be no more prosperous than the local butcher or hardware store owner.

Funeral directors were also protected from too much competition. It was risky to start a new funeral home since, as study after study has shown, when it comes to choosing a funeral home, people are most likely to use the one that their family has used in the past.[1] Even where there was competition, funeral homes did not compete on price. In a submission to the United States Securities Commission, one funeral company boasted of the lack of consumer sensitivity to price increases as one of the bedrock principles of the industry.[2] In the 1960s, the funeral home business was highly fragmented with relatively low profit margins. There were no funeral moguls or corporations. That was all to change. The big story in death over the past twenty-five years has been the rise of a corporate deathcare industry that controls the manufacture of product, the provision of funeral services and the cemetery in which the body is laid to rest. Today, through a process of aggressive expansion two corporations — Service Corporation International (SCI) and Arbor Memorial Services — dominate the Canadian funeral and cemetery business. At the end of 2006, SCI's Canadian operations included 211 funeral homes, four cemeteries, five funeral home/cemetery combinations and twenty crematories. At the same time, Arbor owned ninety-three funeral homes, forty-one cemeteries, twenty-seven crematories and three reception centres (essentially funeral homes located on cemetery land).[3] Two firms dominate the casket industry: Batesville Casket and Matthews International. Together, they constitute Big Death.

SCI AND THE LOEWEN GROUP: A STRUGGLE TO THE DEATH

Robert Waltrip, the man who created the corporate deathcare industry, grew up in a funeral home in Houston, where he realized that most funeral homes were over-capitalized. For example, each had a hearse that might be used only a couple of times a week and an embalming room that might be used only a few hours a week. To cut costs he devised a business model that revolved around the ownership of a cluster of homes in a single market. Once he owned ten to twenty firms in a thirty to sixty mile radius, Waltrip centralized tasks, with one home doing all the embalming, one servicing the vehicles and one doing the accounting. The only thing Waltrip did not change was the sign over the door. The public was not to know that there was a new undertaker in town. People might be willing to abandon the neighbourhood hardware store for True Value and the local grocer for Safeway, but they did not intend to buy a funeral from Service Corporation International — the warm and cuddly name that Waltrip gave to his company. SCI even went so far as to try and register the Family Funeral Care trademark in Canada and the United States. Not surprisingly this move was opposed by family-owned funeral homes, which argued consumers might be misled into thinking they were dealing with a family firm. While SCI successfully registered the trademark in the U.S., it faced ongoing opposition from a variety of organizations of independent funeral homes. In 2002 Canada rejected SCI's registration bid. In recognition of its corporate image, SCI has also sought to develop what it terms the Dignity brand.

Waltrip drove down his costs dramatically, including his labour costs. One study in the mid 1990s said that SCI's fixed costs were 54 percent of revenue, as opposed to 65 percent for the rest of the industry. This sort of market power allowed SCI to negotiate discounts with casket companies and provide its outlets with improved financial services.[4]

Waltrip began adding to his family's two funeral homes in 1962 — the year before the publication of *The American Way of Death* — and in 1968 SCI bought its first Canadian funeral home. By 1992 the company owned over 500 homes including forty funeral homes, two cemeteries and five crematories in Canada. Over the next decade the company mushroomed; in 1999 it owned nearly 4000 funeral homes in twenty countries around the world. It had also gained control of over 500 cemeteries and 200 crematories. Because of their penchant for clustering and buying cemeteries and crematoriums, SCI, along with the Loewen Group and Stewart Enterprises, the funeral industry's big three in the 1990s, were known as consolidators.

SCI's other major innovation was its attempt to crack what the industry terms the "pre-need" market by having people pre-buy their funerals. The pre-need market — people in their fifties and sixties — was a growing percentage of the market in the 1990s. Whoever sold to this group on a pre-need basis in the 1990s would be able to cash in on the golden age of death that will dawn in 2016 when the first baby-boomers turn seventy. SCI salespeople, called family service counselors, were expected to sell at least as much in advance services as they were in sales to people who were in need of immediate services (in the industry, these customers are referred to as "at need" customers). The key to cracking the pre-need market is SCI's Four-S rule: Serve the family, sell the family, solicit referrals, sell referrals.[5]

In 1998, SCI's pre-need cemetery sales accounted for revenues of $450 million. Prearranged funeral contracts sold during the year represent approximately $500 million in revenues that will be realized at some future date, when the services are provided. At the end of 1998, prearranged funeral contracts held by SCI represented nearly $3.7 billion in future revenues to the company.[6] The figure for the Loewen group was $410 million and Stewart Enterprises $819 million. On average there is a twelve-year gap from the time the pre-need contract is sold until the seller has to provide the contracted service. During that period, companies in the U.S. were allowed to either invest the money or use it to buy an insurance policy in the customer's name.[7]

By 2000, SCI owned 25 percent of the Australian industry, 14 percent of the British and 28 percent of the French.[8] Glennys Howarth called this the McDonaldization of funerals, saying services would become "less personal, culturally distinct, and with funeral provision becoming more standardised, individual preferences resisted."[9] The SCI invasion of Australia dates from 1993. It took the company five years and an investment of $250 million to capture 23 percent of the Australian market. By 2001, it was the country's largest funeral provider, with 129 funeral homes, eight cemeteries and fourteen crematories.[10] In 2001, as it sought to reduce its debt, SCI sold 80 percent of its Australian ownings to an Australian-based investor syndicate called InvoCare. In 1994, SCI paid $200 million for the Great Southern Group, the largest British funeral company. SCI also made inroads into the alternative market buying the Neptune Society in San Francisco and First Memorial in British Columbia.[11]

SCI president Robert Waltrip is a friend to both U.S. President George W. Bush and his father, donating $100,000 to the latter's presidential library. These political connections have been important to the company, which has been no stranger to controversy. In the late 1990s Waltrip was involved in a court case arising from charges that, as governor of Texas, George W. Bush put the brakes on a regulatory investigation into SCI's Texas operations. That was only one of a spate of legal problems that the company faced in the last decade.[12]

Two of SCIs biggest problems arose from its efforts to capture the Jewish funeral market in New York City and Florida. In New York City, SCI bought half of the Jewish funeral homes, thereby attracting the attention of high-profile New York State attorney general and future state governor Elliot Spitzer. His investigation concluded that the SCI homes were charging on average 30 to 40 percent more than independent homes. In particular, Spitzer concluded that SCI had entered into agreements with synagogues and large burial societies that required them to identify an SCI home as the society's "official" or "recommended" home. As part of the purchase agreements with SCI, former owners and key employees of the homes that were purchased had to agree not to work in the industry for twenty years. Spitzer's investigation also concluded that SCI would raise casket prices as soon as it bought a home and often stopped selling more modestly priced caskets. In response to Spitzer's investigation, SCI was forced to sell three of its homes and release the former owners and employees from their agreement to stay out of the industry.[13]

SCI's Florida disaster came in 2001, when it was discovered that the company was enhancing revenues at two overcrowded Jewish cemeteries by burying bodies in the wrong places, crushing vaults to create more space and, when all else failed, digging up bodies and tossing them into nearby woods, thus freeing the space for new burials. Aside from the obvious indignity, the desecrations violated Orthodox Jewish teachings that all parts of the body must be buried together. The Florida government launched an investigation and families of those who had been buried at the Menorah Gardens cemeteries in Broward and Palm Beach counties launched lawsuits against SCI. The families claimed that hundreds of bodies had been desecrated because SCI had oversold cemetery space.

In late 2003 one of the civil suits was settled for $100 million, although as 79-year-old Lillian Gruber told the *South Florida Sun-Sentinel*, "I'll never know where my husband is. The thought that he was not allowed to rest in peace, that part is a constant heartbreak that will never be settled." SCI agreed to the settlement to fend off a jury trial of its treatment of the remains of Air Force Colonel Hymen Cohen whose remains had been secretly exhumed and scattered in a nearby wood to make room in the cemetery.[14] SCI was also forced to post a $3-million bond to guarantee that it can resolve the problems at the cemeteries. The company had already agreed to pay $14 million in fines and restitution to the cemeteries. Two SCI employees, including a company vice-president were convicted of misdemeanors. The main reason for dropping the charges was growing concern that SCI insurers would not cover the $100-million class-action settlement if the company were found guilty on the felony charges. If that happened, the state might have been obliged to pick up the tab.[15] The scandal drove the value of SCI stock down from $39 to $3.40.[16]

Such problems were not unique to the United States or to SCI. Arbor Memorial Services, one of the two largest deathcare corporations in Canada, had a brush with ignominy in 2003 when the Alberta government charged it with violating the province's *Fair Trading Act*. At the heart of the case were allegations that the Leyden's Funeral Home in Calgary, which was owned by Arbor, was charging for high-price cremation caskets but in fact cremating people on pieces of scrap wood. A second set of allegations arose out of a complaint that Leyden's had kept a separate, higher price list for Asian clients in anticipation that they would request discounts. According to the government, some fifty-six clients were cheated out of $5000. In some cases it said, people were placed in cremation retorts on plywood retrieved from construction sites. Leyden's former manager Wayne Gorniak was charged with fraud, false pretence and theft. Arbor had fired Gorniak by the time the charges were laid and sent letters to the families offering them a refund for the cremation containers.

A former employee of Leyden's told the *Calgary Herald* how funeral home employees "removed bodies from cremation containers and placed them in either lids or a scrap piece of plywood stored in the car wash bay and put them in the cremation chamber." He said management felt under pressure to cut costs, adding "We would cremate someone on the box and someone else on the lid and save money." The charges against Arbor were eventually withdrawn, but Gorniak pled guilty to having cremated people in partial coffins — sometimes just on the lid — and of inflating the prices quoted to Asian customers over a two-year period. For this he was fined $5750.[17]

Corporate funeral homes are not the only malefactors in the funeral business. The Tri-State Funeral Home in Noble, Georgia, earned its place in the funeral hall of infamy when, in 2001, it was revealed that the family-run home had simply stopped cremating the bodies sent to it, and was, according to one news report, "stockpiling them in vaults, stacking them like cordwood in a building that housed the crematory, unceremoniously dumping the remains in pits and amid piles of trash, or scattering them like discarded mannequins across the crematory compound."[18] In the end, approximately 340 bodies were dumped on the grounds rather than being cremated. Families received urns containing metal, rocks and silica. The crematory had been run by the Marsh family since 1982 — but it had never been licensed or inspected by the Georgia state regulators, who were aware of the crematory's existence. The problem was only identified when the local sheriff was contacted by a man whose dog had unearthed a human skull on a walk near the crematory.

A PRAIRIE BOY'S BRUSH WITH DEATH AND SUCCESS

While Waltrip's SCI dominated the deathcare industry, throughout the 1990s it was given a good run for its money by a country boy from southeastern Manitoba. Until it collapsed in bankruptcy in 1999, the Loewen Group was the second-largest deathcare company in the world. It owned 800 homes and 250 cemeteries and in that year alone spent nearly a billion dollars on new acquisitions, including the purchase of the largest cemetery in North America, Rose Hills Memorial Park in Los Angeles. More than 90 percent of the company's $600 million in revenue came from its U.S. operations. In 1998 Loewen told the Securities Exchange Commission that the company's gross profit margin from funeral operations was 41.5 percent.[19]

Ray Loewen's father ran both the funeral and ambulance services in Steinbach, Manitoba, sixty kilometres from downtown Winnipeg. The family home was next door to the funeral home, and by the time he was fourteen, Ray was driving the ambulance. After attending Briercrest Bible Institute in Saskatchewan, Loewen returned home to take over the family business. Like many rural funeral homes, it provided a modest living charging very modest rates. Ray changed that, raising the prices to match those in Winnipeg. In 1967, he began to branch out, buying a small funeral home in Fort Frances, Ontario. Two years later he jumped into the far more competitive British Columbia market, purchasing a funeral home in New Westminster. Upon moving to B.C., he dabbled in real estate, served as a Social Credit member of the provincial legislature from 1975 to 1979, and then turned his full attention to the funeral industry.[20]

Loewen's expansion was based on two insights. From his own experience he recognized that many family-owned funeral homes were not going to be passed on to the next generation. Secondly, like Waltrip, he recognized that significant economies of scale could be realized by owning several funeral homes in a single market. By 1984 Loewen owned twenty funeral homes in Canada, by 1987 — the year he purchased his first U.S. funeral home — he owned sixty-eight homes in Canada. In 1999 the company owned more than 1100 funeral homes and over 400 cemeteries in Canada and the United States and thirty-two funeral homes in Great Britain.[21]

Loewen claimed that, unlike SCI, he did not micromanage the companies he took over and was reported to allow them considerable autonomy. SCI was even more aggressive than Loewen — indeed, the funeral director who sold Loewen his first U.S. funeral mini-chain had been so turned off by SCI that he said he would burn his homes down rather than sell them to SCI. Loewen was also critical of SCI's high-powered approach to sales and Arbor Memorial's practice of building funeral homes on cemeteries.[22]

Loewen's empire was brought crashing down by what should have been a minor expansion in the heart of the American south. In 1990 Loewen bought Robert Riemann's funeral business in Gulfport, Mississippi, and the Wright & Ferguson funeral home in Jackson, Mississippi. As usual, the Loewen Group instituted a series of measures intended to enhance revenues. Fatefully, head office decreed that henceforth the Wright & Ferguson funeral home would only sell a funeral insurance policy that was owned by the Loewen Group (funeral insurance is one of the instruments that people use to prepay their funerals). This did not sit well with another local funeral director, Jeremiah O'Keefe, who claimed that by contract Wright & Ferguson was obliged to sell his firm's funeral policy — and only his firm's policy. To back up his claim, he sued Riemann and the Loewen Group for breach of contract. Jeremiah O'Keefe was not, it turned out, a man to be trifled with. His grandfather had gone into the funeral business as an expansion of his livery trade at the end of the Civil War. By 1990 this seventy-two-year-old former marine and former mayor owned eight funeral homes in the Biloxi area and many of his thirteen children were employed in the family business. O'Keefe was well regarded by both the white and African-American communities, having once refused to grant the Ku Klux Klan a parade permit when he was mayor of Biloxi. No one could have predicted it at the time, but the ensuing court action, which lasted five years, was to nearly destroy the Loewen Group. It would also provide a fascinating glimpse into what happens when a deathcare corporation comes to town.[23]

Loewen thought a deal could be worked out with O'Keefe in much the same way deals had been worked out in the past, aboard his 110-foot yacht, the Alula Spirit. He had buttered up many a funeral director on board the yacht, anchored in Vancouver's English Bay, as he convinced them to sell the family business. If they did not take to the salmon fishing, he might threaten them with a little hardball. John Wright of the Wright & Ferguson Funeral Home was told that if he did not sell, Loewen intended to build a new funeral home in his territory. Loewen once boasted that this threat made Wright shake so much the coffee sloshed out of his cup. According to journalist Jonathan Harr, "As the chief executive of a growing company, [Loewen] was extroverted, unabashedly garrulous, dictatorial, sometimes quick to anger, and capable of a certain charm when the occasion called for it."[24] When they met on the Alula Spirit, Loewen and O'Keefe reached a tentative agreement under which Loewen would buy three of O'Keefe's homes and O'Keefe would be allowed to continue to sell his policies in all the Loewen homes in Mississippi. But the deal was never consummated. As time dragged one, O'Keefe found himself in a tight financial corner and had to sell off some his homes to another purchaser. And he launched a new lawsuit, accusing Loewen of bad faith and predatory business practices.

When in January 1995 O'Keefe's lawyers offered to settle the case for $4 million, Loewen turned the offer down. His legal team assured him that they would win, and if they lost, the costs would be in the $6 million to $12 million range. Loewen's fate was sealed when O'Keefe hired Willie Gary, a Florida-based personal injury lawyer, who was known for winning his clients multi-million-dollar awards. The son of African-American migrant farm workers, Gary had put himself through university on a football scholarship. A tireless litigator, he was on the road for twenty days a month, travelling across the U.S. in his privately owned plane, the Wings of Justice. His earnings were so good that he had been featured on the *Lifestyles of the Rich and*

Famous television program. Gary would transform the trial from a dry breach of contract dispute into a morality play in which jurors were asked to choose between a foreign corporation that was determined to exploit people in their time of suffering and vulnerability and a small businessman who had served both his community and his country. Where six months earlier O'Keefe had offered to settle the case for $4 million, Gary was now asking for $125 million for his client.

When the trial commenced in the fall of 1995, Gary portrayed Loewen as someone who "would not keep his word, deceived people, and would not deal with honour." He was also trying to "dominate markets, create monopolies, and gouge families that are grieving." For his part, Loewen maintained the deal with O'Keefe had not been finalized because of disagreements over final valuation of the company.[25]

The evidence showed that Loewen used his market power to secure deals from his suppliers that allowed him to undercut his competition. But the savings were not often passed on to the consumer. Loewen introduced a process known as revenue enhancement, which often meant raising prices by 15 percent once he took over a funeral home. In recognition of the third-unit rule — under which purchasers are most likely to choose the second cheapest casket they are shown — funeral homes purchased by Loewen would stop stocking low-priced caskets, nudging customers into higher price brackets.[26]

At the trial it came out that Loewen was selling a burial vault (a protective container in which a casket can be placed and buried in), which he was buying for $940, for $1920 in the Wright & Ferguson Home in Jackson, and for $2860 in his homes in Corinth, Mississippi. Pointing out that the vault was shipped directly from the manufacturer to the cemetery, Gary said, "They charge two thousand eight hundred and sixty dollars, that's almost two thousand dollars for making the phone call. That ain't right. Talking about a monopoly, deceptive trade practices!" Wright, of Wright & Jackson, testified that Loewen had jacked up the rates once he took over his firm. Since becoming a member of the Loewen Group board of directors, Wright said he could not recall a time where the company did not increase prices after taking over a funeral home. A former regional comptroller testified that she had resigned from the Loewen Group because she could no longer support its pricing policies.[27]

To demonstrate its commitment to the African-American community, a Loewen witness presented evidence of a deal that the Loewen Group had recently reached with the National Baptist Convention USA (NBC) to have the church sell Loewen burial plots to church members. Based on a belief that the NBC had eight-million members in 33,000 churches, the Loewen Group believed the deal might be worth up to $400 million a year. Under the deal

Loewen was to train two members from each congregation as funeral counsellors. The pastor was expected to recommend the Loewen Group to any congregation member who needed to arrange for mortuary services, graves and tombstones. In exchange for selling Loewen product, the counsellors got a 10 percent sales commission, the pastor six percent, the congregation five percent and the NBC five percent. Loewen's involvement with the NBC began when he met the church's leader, the Reverend Henry J. Lyons, who became head of the NBC in 1994, and had already made agreements with other corporations for the church to market phone services and credit cards among the African-American community. Soon after Lyons and Loewen first met in 1995, Loewen donated $100,000 to Lyons' Christian Education Fund. Holding out the promise of a meeting with Bill Clinton, Lyons got Loewen to donate another $100,000 to an anti-drug program. This was Loewen's hoped-for route into the African-American funeral market, which was largely served by independent African-American funeral directors.[28]

The deal with Lyons blew up in Loewen's face at the trial. While the Loewen legal team's goal had been to show that the Loewen Group was not a corporate predator but was willing to work with local groups to create jobs for African Americans, Willie Gary successfully portrayed it as an attempt to make $3 billion out of the NBC membership. The seven-week trial ended in disaster for the Loewen Group. The jury not only found for O'Keefe, it came within a single vote of awarding him $1 billion in damages. In the end, they jurors settled on a $500-million award. Up until this case, the largest award in Mississippi civil suit had been $18 million. The Loewen case was not helped when company lawyers claimed the firm was worth $411 million on the same day that a Loewen employee witness valued it at closer to $700 million. Under Mississippi law, Loewen would have had to put up a $625-million bond if he wished to appeal the decision. In the end the company negotiated a $175-million settlement with O'Keefe, who, since he was in his seventies, preferred to see the case wrapped up as quickly as possible.[29]

Loewen's continued involvement with Lyons was to cause him further grief. First, Loewen authorized Lyons to spend up to $2 million investigating suspicions of jury tampering in Mississippi case. Once Loewen settled with O'Keefe, he tried to get Lyons to call off the investigation, only to be told he already spent the $2 million. In the end Loewen paid Lyons $1 million for this work, without ever receiving any receipts.[30]

In July 1997 Lyons' wife set fire to a home belonging to Bernice Edwards, who as police investigating the fire discovered, was Lyons' mistress. Further investigations led them to lay fifty-four charges of racketeering against Lyons. In fifteen of those cases, it was alleged that Lyons had managed to dupe the Loewen Group. In reality, there were only 5000 not 33,000 NBC churches, with 1 million, not 8 million members. According to a *St. Petersburg Times* investigation, "Lyons repeatedly submitted phony expense budgets and then systematically diverted Loewen's funds to himself, his friends, his family, his church and his convention." It turned out that Lyons and his mistress spent the money from Loewen on jewels, private school tuitions, houses, clothing, a private chef, golf equipment, trips to Hawaii and a Mercedes Benz. Not surprisingly, very few burial plots had been sold and very few jobs had been created for church members.[31]

Following the Mississippi decision, SCI offered to buy the Loewen Group for $4.2 billion. Loewen resisted, and regulators across North America indicated that they would launch anti-trust investigations into the implications of any such merger. Loewen also kept on with his acquisition program, paying over $620 million for 159 funeral homes, 136 cemeteries and two insurance companies in 1996.[32] Loewen may have been increasing his company's debt to make SCI think twice about buying the Loewen Group. If this was the strategy, it worked in the short term. In early 1997, SCI dropped its bid, citing concerns about the Loewen Group's debt load, which had hit the $3-billion mark.[33] In 1998, with shares that once sold for forty-two dollars now selling for fifty-three cents, Ray Loewen resigned as chief executive officer. His borrowing and expansion policy had caught up with him: in that year the company lost $599 million.[34]

Loewen was replaced by John Lacey, a corporate turnaround specialist, who had recently negotiated the sale of a Canadian grocery store chain. In June 1999, the Loewen Group filed for bankruptcy protection. The great growth spree was over. By 2002, SCI's president Jerry Pullins acknowledged that the acquisition mania of the 1990s had gotten out of hand.[35] By then SCI was in the process of selling many of its acquisitions at a reduced value. Bidding wars between Loewen, SCI and smaller chains, had led them to over-pay for many of these companies. While Loewen was pushed out of business, SCI was left with a staggering $4.2-billion debt load. There was no cost-cutting in the executive suites however. SCI CEO Robert Waltrip has been a long-time *bête noir* of Graef Crystal, the author of *In Search of Excess*, and scourge of overpaid corporate executives. In 1996 Crystal said that Waltrip's $20.3-million income (which Crystal said was made up of salary, stock and bonuses) made him the twelfth most overpaid executive in the U.S. Given the company's size and performance, Crystal thought Waltrip deserved an annual salary of closer to $2.259 million.[36] When Waltrip's son Blair resigned as company vice-president in 2000, he received payments of $475,000 per year not to go into business in competition with his old man. With stock options, director's fees and other goodies, he received $653,803 in 2001.[37]

In 2002, the Loewen Group emerged from bankruptcy as the Alderwoods Group. While in 2004 it owned 730 funeral homes, 150 cemeteries and sixty combination funeral home and cemetery locations in the United States and Canada, it had sold off many of its holdings — often to the independent operators it bought them from in the first place.[38] In other instances, funeral directors who had sold to Loewen and taken their payment in company shares found themselves forced to go back into the business. By 2004 Alderwoods was once more making money, although it had a debt of $630 million, down two hundred million in two years. Marketing remained a crucial element of the Alderwoods business plan: many of the company's funeral homes were remodeled to accommodate special showrooms for caskets and urns. In response to the rise in cremation and the growing consumer trend not to have any permanent memorial, Alderwoods increased the number of memorial alternatives it marketed, including cremation gardens where people could scatter ashes and have the person's name inscribed on a nearby planter or bench. But Alderwoods was never able to get out from under its debts. In April 2006, Waltrip finally brought down his prey as SCI announced at $856-million takeover of Alderwoods. The combined companies would reportedly have sales of $2.5 billion and control 1712 funeral homes and 490 cemeteries in the United States and Canada.[39]

BIG DEATH'S TIGHT GRIP

The impact of this corporate concentration can be seen across the country. Over a twenty-year period the corporations managed to reduce the number of independent funeral homes in the Montreal area from twenty-eight to six.[40] A federal government study suggests that after a recent merger SCI would have a very significant market share across the country including over 60 percent of the market in Peterborough County, North and West Vancouver, Vancouver and the Fraser River Valley.[41]

Many family funeral home directors continue to harbour a strong dislike of the deathcare corporations. Hewitt Helmsing first entered the funeral industry in 1954 in Regina, establishing his own independent funeral home in 1965. In 1977 he left the industry to head the Saskatchewan Health Care Association, an association of all the provincial hospitals, nursing homes and ambulance boards. While he had sold his funeral home, his name continued to be associated with the business. When Ray Loewen bought the home in the 1990s, he offered Helmsing a share in the firm if he would come back as its manager. Recalls Helmsing, "Initially I thought the rise of corporate funeral homes was positive. It provided an opportunity to get merchandise at a lower rate and to provide some employee benefits, because in the funeral business employee benefits traditionally had been very low." He soon concluded that the corporate homes were driven by a need to improve the return to investors. "Once they bought a funeral home," says Helmsing, "they began to raise the prices. Every other week there seemed to be a price hike to the point where prices were getting out of reach." The crucial moment for Helmsing came when a close friend, whose family he had served in the past, came to him and said,

> "You know my friend, you gouged me. Across the street at the independent I got my uncle's funeral for an awful lot less than you charged me for my mother." I was so embarrassed; my professional integrity was at that point being challenged. I decided I had enough of that life.

He sold his interest in the firm and moved out of the province.

Winnipeg's Neil Bardal says that contrary to their public-relations claims, the conglomerates are not any more efficient than family funeral homes, nor are they less expensive. Bardal continues,

> But their marketing is very good. They have the resources to make the telephone calls. They have the resources to do good advertising and the sales force is out there. The main players in the corporations are accountants, and they are not innovative and they do not want to be. They will take somebody else over if they are successful, but they are not going to break any new ground. They hire nice people, they have pristine facilities. But they are not price competitive.

He thinks that the family funeral home will only be rarer and rarer over time. He adds, "It simply costs too much to come into this business. If you are successful or develop a new approach, the conglomerates will come along and buy you. If they can't do that, they will copy you."

THE CASKET MAKERS

Batesville, Indiana, is to caskets what Detroit used to be to automobiles — the productive heart of the industry. If Detroit is the Motor City, this is Casket Town. A third of North America's caskets come from a company with its headquarters in this all-but-unknown community. The 675 workers employed by the Batesville Casket Company plant in Batesville turn out a thousand caskets each day. And the company has four more plants in four other states, supplying over 16,000 funeral homes with over 500 styles and colours of caskets that can be embellished with one of over 15,000 separate interior designs. Aside from religious designs, draped with different shades and fabrics, one can buy theme caskets for virtually every hobby or enthusiasm. The Batesville Casket's annual sales are $650 million, triple that of its closest competitor, Matthews International, owner of both the York and Milsco casket lines.

Batesville has its own version of the Alula Spirit, a 657-acre retreat called Jawacdah Farms, near Batesville. Funeral directors are flown here for gourmet meals and seminars. Calvin Corson of the Kaiser-Corson Funeral Homes of Iowa told *Forbes Magazine*, "It's an awesome experience… On a trip like that you take away more than you leave. It's never 'How can we sell caskets?' but 'How can we improve your life, business and the customers you serve?'" The company has two 1000-square-foot traveling casket showrooms. At no charge, the company also builds showrooms for its caskets in funeral homes. Not surprisingly, many funeral directors agree to sell only Batesville products.[42]

As late as 1950 there were over 700 casket companies in the United States with over 20,000 employees. Over half of all the caskets sold were cloth-covered boxes, usually softwoods. But from the 1950s onward there were two key trends in the industry: the rise of steel caskets and the concentration of manufacturing. Thanks to the development of a ready supply of inexpensive steel, the industry shifted to steel caskets, often with a gasket seal. Batesville led this trend, switching to metal caskets after World War I. By the 1970s two-thirds of the caskets sold were metal. Where once every company made cloth-covered caskets, today, only a few companies do so, largely for the local market. Since it cost millions to purchase the grinding, stamping, welding, sanding and painting equipment to make metal caskets, many of the small companies fell by the wayside. Meanwhile, the number of casket manufacturers fell to 523 in 1967, to 211 in 1992 and to 177 in 1997. During the same period, employment in the industry dropped from 16,800 to 7800 to 6962. This consolidation took place at the same time that cremation was increasing. As a result, even with a reduction in the number of casket companies, the industry has more production capacity than customers.[43]

Forbes estimate that the U.S. casket industry is worth about $1.4 billion a year, and there is no doubt that the caskets remain the single most expensive component of funeral costs.[44] We have come a long way from the winding sheet or the pine box. There are essentially three different types of caskets sold for traditional funerals: cloth-covered, hardwood caskets (including caskets that have hardwood veneers) and metal caskets (steel, copper, or bronze). Cloth-covered caskets are usually made from softwoods, pressed wood or fibreboard and covered with cloth.

In recent years in the United States there have been a number of legal challenges to the market control exercised by the casket corporations. The U.S. Federal Trade Commission (FTC) Casket Rule, requiring funeral homes to allow customers to supply their own caskets, led to the rise of direct-sale casket retailers such as FuneralDepot.com and enticed Costco into the casket business. The savings that these retailers offer can be significant: a Batesville top of the line Promethean Bronze casket might sell for $25,000 at a funeral home, but can be had for as little as $6750 at a direct seller. Until the casket rule came into place, it had been common for funeral homes in the U.S. to prohibit customers from supplying their own casket. Even with the rule in place Batesville will not sell to direct-sale casket retailers, saying that it will sell only to licensed funeral homes.[45] While funeral directors have lobbied state legislatures to pass laws that prohibit anyone but a funeral director from selling caskets, the U.S. courts have regularly struck down these laws as unnecessary restrictions on trade. Attempts by funeral directors to impose casket-handling fees have also been struck down by the courts. In one case, the judge found that the funeral parlour was telling customers, "either buy our casket here, or we'll charge you for it anyway."[46]

In May 2004 the Funeral Consumers Alliance (FCA), which is the national association of U.S. memorial societies, and six families filed a lawsuit against SCI, Alderwoods and Stewart Enterprises, along with the Batesville Casket Company, claiming that in violation of U.S. antitrust laws the defendants had conspired to keep casket prices high and shut out low-cost casket sellers. This policy allowed the deathcare corporations to sell caskets for up to six times their wholesale price. According to the suit, the funeral industry has boycotted casket manufacturers who supply the discounters.[47] The FCA statement of claim argues that following the imposition of the casket rule, the big three began pressuring Batesville to continue to sell only to licensed funeral directors. According to the FCA, if Batesville discovered that a funeral home was selling caskets to an independent casket dealer, it would threaten to stop supplying that firm with caskets. In some cases funeral homes placed orders on behalf of independent casket companies, requesting that the casket be delivered to the funeral home actually performing the service. When this occurred, the funeral home making the order charged a small mark up, but the cost to the customer was still less than what a funeral home would have charged.

To stop this, Batesville began insisting that the company that received the casket be the company that was billed for the casket. A survey of funeral homes for *Funeral Service Insider* magazine showed that

> One-third of our respondents say they've pulled their business from casket or vault suppliers who deal with third-party seller — and nearly one-fifth say they've gone even further: They've urged other funeral homes to boycott suppliers who deal with third party sellers.

Funeral Monitor quoted an SCI representative as saying,

> Funeral consumers have returned to us after funerals and questioned us about the price we charged them for a particular casket. In many cases they have gone on the Internet and found the same casket we

sold them priced as much as 60 percent less than we charged....
[T]o prevent consumers from comparing apples to apples, we have
asked Batesville to stop selling their caskets to casket stores and
Internet vendors."[48]

For its part, Batesville has argued that it is restricting sales to funeral home to
ensure that its product is used with the dignity that the company intended.
According to *USA Today*, a Connecticut man who inquired as to whether
he could provide a casket purchased through the Internet was told by his
funeral director that "those things are made by prisoners," while a different
funeral director responded, "I'm sorry we don't have any tin cans for you
to look at."[49]

The FTC has recognized that some funeral homes have discount strategies that essentially serve as reverse handling fees to discourage the use of
independent casket suppliers. According to the FTC:

> For example, the prices of itemized goods and services (appearing
> on the General Price List) may in some instances be inflated to the
> point of fictitiousness. Thus, virtually all consumers would choose
> to purchase "discount packages," resulting in a situation where the
> discount package represents the de facto prices for the goods and
> services. Such a scenario may restrict consumer choice in a man-
> ner that frustrates the intended purpose of the Rule. Further, some
> members of the funeral industry have alleged that because such
> "discount packages" are often conditioned on the purchase of a
> casket, these packages are artificially constructed by certain funeral
> providers in order to eliminate competition in casket sales.[50]

The Funeral Consumers Alliance case against the deathcare conglomerates
was set to go to trial in early 2008.

The casket corporations have a strong interest in how its products are
marketed. In the late 1980s, twenty-five years after the publication of *The
American Way of Death*, the Batesville Casket Company commissioned U.S.
marketing expert Alton F. Doody to prepare a study on funeral-home marketing. Doody, who had worked for a variety of department stores in the
past, claims he was astounded by what he encountered. Says Doody, "From
a merchandising management viewpoint, it is as if I had walked into a time
capsule! Here was an entire industry operating in the 1980s at the level
of retail merchandising of the 1880s; kind of on par with the old general
store."[51]

Most places showed only fifteen to twenty caskets and, according to
Doody, everything else was marketed in a haphazard way. Markups varied
dramatically from two to five times higher than cost. The potential loss to the

funeral home was significant, since Doody estimates that 50 to 60 percent of a funeral home's revenue comes from the sale of funeral-related products.[52]

Doody thought that the homes did not display enough product (a conclusion that could only have pleased his casket-manufacturing sponsor) and that they did not organize them into coherent lines. He recommended that a forward-looking company would stock at least forty styles and would organize them into product lines and tiers of good better and best and that pricing reflect this breakdown. Because the names assigned to caskets should reflect the place the different caskets occupy in their array of merchandise, Doody encouraged funeral directors to drop the names that the casket companies gave their products, and to give them new names:

> Names assigned to high-end units should be descriptive of high-end places or personages, such as President, Monarch, Senator, Congressional, or the like. Names assigned to middle-priced units, should be descriptive of fine things or paces, such as Bentley, Carlton, Carlisle, Hyde Park, or the like. Names assigned to lower-priced units should be more nondescript, such as Fairlane, Abbey, Huntley, or the like.[53]

There is, of course, another very good reason why funeral directors might wish to rename their products: it makes it nearly impossible for customers to comparison shop. As Doody notes with satisfaction, "Since it is unlikely that you will have exactly the same price as your competitor, you can avoid the matter altogether by assigning your own names to the merchandise that you sell."[54] It is, he says, perfectly legal. Given that Doody regularly argues that he is out to make life better for both the funeral director and the customer, it is revealing that in this case, he recommended a policy that actively frustrates customers.

Prices of these renamed caskets ought to be aligned, not with the cost of the casket, but with the three distinct lines that the funeral home should try to develop. The low-price line prices would be between $500 and $2000, the mid-line between $2000 and $3750 and the high-end line between $3750 and $7000. He terms these logical progressions of value that allow consumers to identify the differences in value between the caskets.[55] The logic is, of course, arbitrary, and the value to the funeral director is to increase prices.

As the preceding suggests, the path to death's dark door does not run smoothly. The old family-run funeral homes that Jessica Mitford held up for public ridicule have been dealt a one-two punch by the corporate consolidators and by the growing trend away from the traditional funeral. As a result, even though the local funeral parlour or cemetery may have a familiar name hanging over the door, you could well be dealing with a corporation. Even if you call several funeral homes in an effort to shop around for a better deal you could be dealing with the same corporate owners. There is no free funeral, but there ought to be some way to assure that you or your heirs don't get skinned. There are reasons for hope. There are local funeral directors who are attempting to recover their trade's good name, either through cost-cutting or innovation. There are also organizations and people who soldier on in the hope of ensuring the funeral consumer gets a better deal.

CHAPTER 5

INVENTING NEW
FUNERAL TRADITIONS

IF YOU GO TO A FUNERAL HOME TODAY, YOU are likely to be told that your two main choices are a traditional funeral or cremation. In his cultural history of the funeral trade, Gary Laderman defines the traditional funeral as the "removal of the body from the home or hospital, embalming and preparing it in the funeral home, displaying the deceased in the casket before and/or during services in the chapel, and transportation to the grave."[1] Critics of the traditional funeral are usually quick to point out there is nothing that traditional about this sort of funeral, going on to argue that it is an invention of funeral directors, casket companies and cemetery owners. Certainly, no one as recently as one hundred and fifty years ago spoke of having a traditional funeral, they just expected that their bodies would be disposed of in the way that people in their part of the world had disposed of bodies for centuries. Historian Eric Hobsbawm points out that it is only after old relationships and traditions have been broken down by industrialism and the market that people start inventing traditions to give their constantly changing lives a sense of continuity.[2]

Taking the long view, we can see dramatic changes in the way human beings care for and memorialize their dead. As a species, we have not done a very good job of memorializing those who went before us. While archeologists believe the first ceremonial burial took place about 120,000 years ago, it is estimated that we have memorialized only about 0.01 percent of the 100 billion human beings who have died in just the past 10,000 years.[3] If cremation and scattering seem less than respectful, consider that Neanderthals and early humans may well have eaten their dead. According to archeologist Timothy Taylor, this was an inherited primate behaviour that was transformed into a way to control the dead. It existed in both a militant form, in which warriors ate their slain enemies, and in a reverential form, in which survivors hoped to channel and absorb the spirit of dead ancestors. In the Neolithic farming community of Catalhoyuk in what is now Turkey, 7200 years ago people lived in houses made of plaster and mudbrick, with each house abutting the next one. When a home deteriorated, a new one was built on top of the old one. When a member of the community died, the body was wrapped in a mat and lowered into a hole dug in the floor. Aside from Cary Grant's dotty but deadly aunts in the 1944 movie *Arsenic and Old Lace* (who had their victims buried in their basement), this is a tradition that most of us are probably happy to have turned our backs on.

In early human society burial was intended to ensure that the soul of the deceased did not reanimate the body. This was done by keeping the departed soul away from the body until it decomposed. In some societies, if you held the wrong social status, you might find yourself being buried as a bit player in someone else's funeral. One would want to stay well away from the traditional funeral of a Scythian king. According to the Greek historian Herodotus, after placing the embalmed king in a burial pit, the Scythians "bury one of his concubines, after strangling her, and his wine-bearer, cook, groom, steward, and his message-bearer."[4]

Those of us who believe that the state funerals given to such notables as Pierre Trudeau, Princess Diana and John F. Kennedy are part of a timeless tradition would be surprised by historian David Cannadine's observation that:

> The majority of the great royal pageants staged during the first three-quarters of the nineteenth century oscillated between farce and fiasco. In 1817, at the funeral of Princess Charlotte, the daughter of the Prince Regent, the undertakers were drunk. When the duke of York died, ten years later, the chapel at Windsor was so damp that most of the mourners caught cold, Canning contracted rheumatic fever and the bishop of London died.

After talking throughout much of the funeral of George IV, William IV walked out of the service, an event on which the *Times* commented, "We never saw so motley, so rude, so ill-managed a body of persons." William's own funeral was described as a "wretched mockery."[5] The late nineteenth century marked the opening the golden age of the state funeral: the funerals of the Italian King Victor Emmanuel II in 1878, Russian Czar Alexander III in 1894, German Kaiser Wilhelm I in 1888 and England's Queen Victoria in 1901 were all major exhibitions of pomp and grandeur. A tradition had been invented.

For a variety of reasons, people are continuing to invent new funeral traditions. Some, like the green funeral, marry the concern with overly ostentatious funerals to a more contemporary environmental critique of the "traditional" funeral. In other cases, people have created cooperatives or joined memorial societies in an effort to regain control of funeral costs and what they viewed as an increasingly commercialized experience.

THE GREEN FUNERAL

Both the traditional funeral and cremation are vulnerable to environmental critiques. Memorial parks are in essence gigantic lawns that need to be fertilized, watered and regularly maintained — almost always with gasoline-powered equipment. The parks undermine biological diversity, consume vast amounts of energy and resources, and dump nutrients that can pollute waterways into the environment. Beneath these fields are buried marvels of modern technology: expensive woods, buffed metals, elaborate seals and gaskets, often shipped from hundreds if not thousands of miles away and often wrapped in concrete liners. These cemeteries are designed to prevent the human body doing what the body of every other organism eventually does — decompose.

While cremation rapidly returns the body to dust, it requires twenty litres of natural gas and releases a variety of metals into the air. The issue of greatest concern is the release of mercury into the atmosphere. The mercury, which comes from dental fillings, is released into the air upon cremation. Cremated human remains are 47.5 percent phosphate, 25.3 percent calcium, 11 percent sulphate, 3.7 percent potassium, 1.12 percent sodium, 1 percent chloride, .9 percent silica and 0.72 percent aluminum oxide.[6]

Given that cremated ashes are nearly 50 percent phosphate, they can act as a fertilizer, somewhat akin to the bone meal some gardeners use. Continued scattering of ash in one place can have an impact on soil and vegetation. In the United Kingdom, the Mountaineering Council of Scotland has asked members of the public not to scatter ashes on Ben Nevis, the tallest mountain in the U.K., and other Scottish summits because plants that thrive on the increased phosphorous were overrunning the mountains' natural vegetation.[7]

The European Union has led the way in regulating these emissions. In Britain it is expected that by 2010 cremation will be the single largest contributor of airborne mercury in the country, while in Sweden one-third of airborne mercury comes from crematories. In 2005 the British government introduced regulations intended to cut mercury emissions in half by 2020.[8] Much of this will be achieved by allowing companies with more efficient technology to sell credits to companies that are less efficient.[9]

North American regulation is far less stringent. Research carried out for the U.S. Environmental Protection Agency (EPA) at a New York crematory found that emissions of smoke, particulates, carbon monoxide, nitrogen, sulfur dioxide, hydrogen chloride, metals (cadmium, mercury, lead), dioxins and furans increased with the temperature used in the retort. The EPA was not alarmed by the level of emissions, and, based on the research carried out at this single crematory, assigned crematories a very low regulatory priority and introduced no special regulations for crematories.[10]

There currently is little regulation of emissions from Canadian crematories, which, following the U.S. approach, are considered low-risk operations. In 1997 the British Columbia government called on Service Corporation International to cease emissions at its Saanich crematory because residents were complaining about contamination from smoke from the crematory. Although the company initially challenged the government's authority to issue such an order, it decided to upgrade its equipment.[11] Nevertheless, a decade later, residents were still complaining about emissions from the crematory, which the company states is monitored and adjusted in the case of problems. In 2006, the B.C. Interior Health Authority recommended against locating a crematory in a residential district of Kamloops because there is so little environmental regulation of the industry.[12] At the same time the province's chief medical health officer said the government should consider requiring that crematories be licensed under the *Environmental Management Act*.[13]

In England, environmental concerns have led to the growth of a natural burial or green burial movement. Other terms for a green cemetery include woodland cemetery, nature reserve burial ground, eco-cemetery, memorial grove, green graveyard or garden of remembrance. The non-profit Natural Death Centre was established in 1991 to "support those dying at home and their carers, and to help people arrange inexpensive, family-organised, and environmentally-friendly funerals."[14] According to the centre there are now over 200 existing or planned natural burial grounds in England, usually located on farms or woodlots. Bodies are buried in a wooded spot in wooden coffins, wicker baskets or shrouds. In many cases, families plant trees over the grave. In others, the body is laid at the foot of an existing tree. In either case, a record is kept of the location and occupant of each grave.[15] By 2010 the centre expects a tenth of all British funerals to be woodland funerals. There have been a few attempts to establish green cemeteries in the United States, but the largest of these, Fernwood in California, is under corporate ownership, and with some grave sites selling for upwards of $30,000 dollars, can hardly been seen to as a union of economy and simplicity.[16] While the natural death movement is relatively recent, many readers are likely to have realized it is simply adopting elements of both Jewish and Islamic traditions that call for unembalmed burial in shrouds or unadorned wooden boxes.

Jane Saxby, the cemeteries administrator for the City of Winnipeg, is hoping that one day a natural burial ground will be founded in Manitoba. A former cemetery administrator in England, Saxby is well aware of the growth of the natural-death movement in Britain, where she says "there are, in effect, different levels of naturalness. A true green cemetery will do interments only in a biodegradable casket. That usually means a cardboard casket, which may sound not very nice, but in fact they are often quite good looking. Other people also buy wicker caskets. Others will only inter bodies in shrouds made of silk, since silk dissolves much more quickly than cotton.

Some cemeteries will not allow any markers while others might allow a tree or a small wooden marker, but once it deteriorates they will not allow it to be replaced. Some allow the presence of cremated remains, other do not."

North Americans television viewers were introduced to the natural-death concept in the finale of the television series *Six Feet Under*, in which Nate Fisher, the co-owner of the funeral home featured in the program, is given a green funeral. In a piece of product placement that suggests that the green funeral need not be an unmarketed funeral, Nate went to meet his maker wrapped in a Kinkara shroud. According to Kinkara's website, these shrouds are made of "completely natural silks, cottons, linens, wools and Antique fabrics featuring a 100% cotton batting hand-sewn lining with a strong canvas back." The three styles (Purelight, Botanika Restspa and Royal Deity) come in four sizes, have wooden slats sewn into their backs and can be accessorized with the Endfinity Knot lowering device. Like a number of European firms, the company markets a series of biodegradable coffins.[17]

Canada has no green cemeteries. In his 2002 thesis on the feasibility of woodland cemeteries in Canada, Michael Salisbury identified two routes to establishing a successful woodland cemetery in Canada. The first, convert-ing an existing woodlot, would protect the woodlot from being cleared and have the advantage of being pre-treed. However, because it is pre-treed, the cemetery would fill up more quickly, would not allow the use mechani-cal digging equipment, which could damage tree roots, and any memorial trees planted by families would run the risk of being stunted by the existing forest canopy. The alternative is to create a new woodlot, often by restoring an environmentally damaged site. This would allow a more efficient design and a higher density of graves. It would not necessarily look like a natural forest, particularly if families were permitted to plant non-native trees. There is also the risk that such a cemetery would resemble an artificial tree farm.

Salisbury proposes the creation of a series of circular burial forests, each thirty metres across, with a memorial stone garden at the centre. Marked stones (not headstones) would match the location of unmarked graves in the burial forest. The garden at the centre of the forest could also serve as a setting for memorial and committal services. Such developments, he writes, could be added to existing cemeteries. And although the land usage is not as efficient as in a lawn cemetery, the cemetery could achieve significant reductions in maintenance costs. In the same way that the rural cemetery was once seen as a source of moral uplift, green cemetery proponents argue that they can assist the bereaved by placing death in the context of larger life processes and simultaneously recognizing that cemeteries can serve mixed usages.[18]

Salisbury is a founding member of the Natural Burial Cooperative,[19] which was launched on Earth Day, April 22, 2006. The cooperative's long-range goal is to establish a series of natural burial cemeteries across the country that would also market environmentally safe burial products. In early 2007, it stated that it was negotiating with a landowner to establish its first Ontario cemetery. Salisbury is quite pleased by the response to the cooperative so far. He adds,

> Right now we have over one hundred members. And while the cost of a lifetime membership is quite low at $25, it is important to remember that right now we cannot really offer people any benefits. People are investing because this is something that they really want to see happen.

In British Columbia, the Royal Oak Burial Park, a non-profit cemetery in Saanich on Vancouver Island also has plans to establish a green burial site.[20]

Natural cemeteries offer a number of potential savings. For example, there are no monument costs, most shrouds are considerably cheaper than caskets and maintenance is limited. However, there are no guarantees that is would necessarily be cheaper. Factors that would determine costs include the cost of establishing and operating the cemetery and the features included in the cemetery — for example, digging graves manually is potentially more expensive than digging them with a backhoe.

A natural burial ground need not be treed at all. In places where the natural terrain is tall grass prairie, a treed burial ground could hardly be called natural. While the Cemeteries Branch of the City of Winnipeg is only investigating the possibility of introducing a natural burial site, cemeteries administrator Saxby suggests the area could be a prairie grass cemetery setting. Says Saxby, "A natural cemetery would contribute to creating a prairie-land ecology. At a ceremony, for example, you could give people native grass seeds to scatter over the lot." She sees it as a way of increasing people's options for an interment. Saxby says that the city would not establish such a cemetery without extensive planning, including a public consultation to see if people are interested in and understand this alternative type of internment.

One of the points that Saxby stresses is that if it established a natural interment area, the city would continue to keep track of where each person were buried as it currently does with all interments within city-operated cemeteries. A natural burial ground would probably include a rule preventing any disinterment. One can still have a natural burial, even if it is not in a natural burial ground. Saxby says that some people are buried in Winnipeg cemeteries without markers and she would consider accommodating someone who wished to be buried in a shroud.

PROMESSION

Strict European environmental laws have led a Swedish community to take the latest step in the evolution of the disposition of human remains — freeze-drying. The southern Swedish town of Jönköping plans to replace its aging crematorium with the world's first promatorium in 2008. In the promatorium, bodies are freeze-dried by dipping them in liquid nitrogen. A gentle wave vibration is then used to shatter the body into powder, from which any liquids and metals are removed. The remaining powder is placed in a biodegradable container and interred in a shallow grave, where it can serve as compost to a memorial tree. Swedish biologist Susanne Wiigh-Masak is the driving force behind this process, which she refers to as "promession." According to Wiigh-Masak, "Mulching was nature's original plan for us, and that's what used to happen to us at the start of humanity — we went back into the soil." Jönköping turned to this method because it is expected to be much cheaper than installing the sort of gas-cleaning system and furnace that would be required to meet current environmental standards.[21]

MEMORIAL SOCIETIES AND COOPERATIVES

For over a half a century, memorial societies have sought to provide North American consumers with low-cost funeral alternatives. As described earlier, they grew out of the Unitarian Church and its concern with the growing expense and opulence of funerals. From the outset, they sought to join simplicity and dignity with economy. Fired by Jessica Mitford's *The American Way of Death*, they experienced considerable growth during the 1960s. In most communities where they exist, memorial societies negotiate base price funerals for their members with one or more local funeral directors. Neil Bardal recalls that when the Winnipeg branch of the memorial society was established in 1956 his father got into a conflict with Unitarian minister Phil Petursson ("Icelanders love to argue," sighs Bardal). As a result, the Mordue Brothers funeral home got all of the society's business.

Memorial societies have always met with resistance from the funeral industry. When two university professors established a memorial society in Saskatchewan in the 1960s, they had a hard time finding a funeral home that was willing to deal with them. Eventually they contacted Regina funeral director Hewitt Helmsing, who agreed to provide service to society members at a set fee. According to Helmsing, "The first thing I knew, the society had signed up several thousand people from across the province." His fellow funeral directors were initially furious with him, but eventually a number of them began to do business with the society as well. Hemsing was relieved by this development, since he was far from certain that his funeral home would be able to service all of the society's members. At the time there was no cremation in Saskatchewan, so the main service Helmsing offered the society was burial in a simple container with no embalming.

Memorial societies usually charge a one-time membership fee in the twenty- to forty-dollar range and have lists of what they call cooperating funeral homes that provide service at reduced prices to society members. For example, according to its website the Memorial Society of Northern Ontario (based in Sudbury) has contracts with a number of funeral homes to provide two types of funerals for a set price range. The Type A funeral, at a cost of $750 to $1200, includes removal of the body, completion of necessary paperwork, a plain casket or container and transportation to the cemetery or crematory. There is no embalming, viewing or funeral procession. Type B, at a cost of $1300 to $1650, includes a visitation and service, but no embalming or viewing. In both cases, crematory and cemetery charges are in addition to these fees.[22] Other societies negotiate a set rate with the provincial funeral directors association that all members are to be charged for specific funerals. In Canada, memorial societies of some form exist in Montreal and every province west of the Ottawa River, but have not managed to put down roots in the rest of Quebec or the Atlantic Provinces.

The crown jewel among North American memorial societies is the Memorial Society of British Columbia. As described in Chapter 2, in the 1950s, when the British Columbia funeral industry refused to have anything to do with the memorial society, Doug Foreman established First Memorial, a privately owned funeral home to provide services to society members. Between them, the Memorial Society of British Columbia and First Memorial kept provincial funeral prices among the lowest in the country. With 200,000 members, the society is still the continent's largest memorial society but has had to come to terms with unanticipated consequences of its close relationship with First Memorial. That relationship was positive as long as First Memorial was owned by either Doug Foreman or his family members. But in 1989, several years after Foreman's death, the family sold the firm to SCI. At the time of purchase, First Memorial had a contract that gave it the exclusive right to supply funeral services to the society (with the exception of those locations with no First Memorial outlet). Members could always go elsewhere, but the society could not sign agreements with other homes if there was a First Memorial outlet in the community. At the time of the purchase by SCI, the contract was set to run until 1996. However, in the early 1990s, SCI, citing its long-term planning needs, asked the society to agree to extend the contract to 2006. In a decision it would come to regret, the society agreed.

The society soon discovered that its contract with First Memorial was very loose; indeed, the contract did not set out the prices of most of the elements of a funeral. This had not mattered in the past, since Foreman and his family always operated in a manner that reflected the society's approach. However, under SCI's management, prices that were outside the contract were increased.

As a result, when society members died, they were no longer getting the cheapest funerals in the province. No one, it should be noted, has suggested that there was anything illegal in SCI's decision to raise those prices.

Furthermore, First Memorial under SCI was taking a far more aggressive approach to marketing its services that it had in the past. One of the benefits that First Memorial had provided to its early customers was its "no hassle, no haggle" policy. When I met with the society's executive director Walter Johanson in his Vancouver office in March 2006, he was livid about what he saw as a recent attempt to pre-sell a funeral to a society member. A week earlier, the member phoned to tell him she just received a call from someone claiming to be a society representative who wanted to drop by in a week's time to update membership information. Johanson told her that the society was not undertaking any such update and that it was likely a funeral home trying to get her to pre-buy her funeral. What happened next was, according to Johanson, like a scene out of a movie. As Johanson describes,

> The woman was outraged. She arranged to have her neighbour keep watch from the front street and get the license plate number of the car, while her husband hid in the backyard to take pictures of whoever showed up. When someone from the funeral home drove up and knocked on the door, our member said she was too sick to meet with the caller, the salesperson dropped off a First Memorial business card and a First Memorial planning guide. She did not drop off any society form that needed updating.

Calling this sort of activity "an unethical sales tactic used to gain access to the homes of the vulnerable," Johanson said, "Yesterday is a typical example of what has been going on, except that we finally hammered them. We have had a lot of complaints about SCI, but they always say that is not a policy of our company." When Johanson complained about the call, the investigating police officer asked him, "Why are you still dealing with this company if you have so many complaints?" It was a question that society members were asking themselves.

The Memorial Society of British Columbia's contract with First Memorial was set to expire in September 2006, presenting the society with a dilemma. Even if it did not renew the agreement, many members might continue to go to First Memorial, since they associated it so closely with the society. SCI was counting on that connection; in a meeting with First Memorial executives, one of the managers told Johanson, "We consider the Memorial Society a sub-brand of First Memorial Funeral Homes." Breaking away from First Memorial would also hurt the society financially, since under the contract it received a "records-holding fee" from every member who went to First Memorial and it would lose that revenue on all the members who continued to erroneously use First Memorial. As Johanson put it, "We have the moral dilemma about what to do with the fox — keep an eye on him or let him run loose."

In the end, the memorial society broke loose. In the fall of 2006, it announced a new list of providers, all of which were local, Canadian-owned funeral homes. Johanson said the new contract, which was much more detailed than the previous agreement, could lower costs by as much as 30 percent.[23] Johanson believes that the society can once more play an important role in protecting British Columbia funeral consumers. For example, it is exploring ways to increase the services it provides, including the provision of memorial society branded coffins and urns. Johanson is cool on the idea of funeral prepayment, noting, "In many ways you are probably better off saving your money in a mutual fund." However, since many society members do prepay their funerals, he said the society is looking into considering proposals from insurance companies. In reviewing the events, Johanson said, "We account for 20 percent of the funerals in the province. We are going to start to throw our weight around, gently. I hope this gentle aggressiveness will bode for better."

A COOPERATIVE APPROACH

Steinbach, Manitoba, a little more than a half-hour drive southeast of Winnipeg, is Ray Loewen's hometown. The family funeral business is still in operation, although in the summer of 2006 it was owned and operated by the Alderwoods Group (which had just been sold to SCI). Steinbach is also the heart of Manitoba's Mennonite community, the setting for Miriam Toews's much-honoured *A Complicated Kindness*. It is also home to one of the most successful challenges to the world of corporate deathcare. In the mid-1990s, Elbert Toews, a retired school principal in Steinbach, was one of a number of people concerned by "the monopoly funeral business in the Steinbach area" and, as he says,

> [the] exorbitantly high prices they were charging. Locally you would hear that what cost $5000 a few years ago was now costing close to $10,000. A group of us felt we could do better. We had some inside information on what funerals cost and we believed that you could charge a reasonable fee and not lose money. But we felt that the corporations could take out any small private enterprise. As a result, we thought the most effective way to organize was to establish a cooperative.

In November 1996 Toews and a handful of other local residents began laying the groundwork for the Birchwood Funeral Chapel, one of the few cooperatively owned funeral homes in North America.

They started selling memberships in the cooperative in late May 1997 and within five weeks five hundred people had come up with the $200 membership fee. By time the cooperative broke the sod for a funeral chapel in October 1997 it had 1700 members. According to Toews, shortly after it went into full operation in May 1998, "We brought the price of a funeral down by a couple of thousand dollars. As a result, we have basically taken over 80 percent of the regional market." Toews says the cooperative is not engaging in low-ball pricing to drive out the competition. He adds, "If a private entrepreneur set up in town and charged what we charged, they could make a decent living. Our intent was to take out the corporation that was gouging people."

In the summer of 2006 the cooperative had 2700 members. The building, valued at $1 million (mortgage-free since 2004), is comparable to many of the corporate funeral homes in a large urban centre, complete with a chapel, reception area, display room, preparation area and large parking lot. The only service that it contracts out is cremation. In 2004, Birchwood opened up a storefront operation in northeast Winnipeg, and while it has not penetrated the Winnipeg market in the same way that it has taken off in southeastern Manitoba, it has over 700 Winnipeg-area members.

Toews said, "You do not have to be a member to be a customer of Birchwood. The prices we charge non-members are lower than those charged by corporate funeral homes." Membership provides several additional advantages: first of all, the initial membership fee is credited to the cost of the member's eventual funeral. Secondly, members receive a 20 percent discount on the funeral service fee (the discount does not apply to goods such as caskets). Finally, any profits are returned to each member's account in the form of a dividend. In recent years this has amounted to a 5 to 10 percent annual return on investment. The value of these dividends is eventually deducted from the cost of the members' funeral. The cooperative links to community are also demonstrated by the fact it can draw on a network of 75 volunteers to assist at funerals. It is also the sort of place that serves borscht all day long at its annual open house.

The Birchwood Funeral Home is not the only funeral cooperative in Canada, but they are relatively rare phenomenon. Its success is due, at least in part, to the strength of the general dissatisfaction with the local corporate funeral home, a lack of low-cost alternatives and a community tradition of self-help. It remains to be seen if they will enjoy the same success in larger, more anonymous urban settings. The ongoing existence of memorial societies and funeral cooperatives underscores the fact that many Canadians are wary of the funeral industry. Those Canadians who do not seek out such protection are dependent on government regulation to protect their interests. They are leaning on a particularly weak reed.

CHAPTER 6

"IF IT ISN'T ETHICAL, IT PROBABLY ISN'T GOING TO BENEFIT THE CONSUMER"
REGULATING THE FUNERAL INDUSTRY

O N FEBRUARY 8, 2007, CBC TELEVISION in Winnipeg ran a story about a woman who had been hit with a $4000 bill for her husband's funeral. While this was not an unusually high bill, the woman had thought the fee would be in the $1500 range. In a state of shock, she had signed a contract for $4000 worth of services. Later, when she realized that the Canada Pension Plan was providing only a $2500 death benefit, she tried to switch to another funeral home. But by then the first funeral home had cremated the body and would not release the ashes until it had been paid $2900. When the widow did not pay, the funeral home owner took her to small claims court, where the bill was reduced to $2100.[1]

The day after the broadcast, I was having lunch with Norm Larsen and Neil Bardal. As the vice-chair of the provincial committee that regulates the funeral industry, Bardal was familiar with the case. His sympathies were with the widow, but he also realized that the funeral director in question had done nothing that violated the existing funeral industry regulations. She had been drawn to the funeral home initially because it advertises "a service of remembrance for $1500." She did not realize that this service did not include disposition of the body — that would be extra. Bardal said, "It is like the two-dollar-and-fifty-cent breakfasts that some restaurants advertise. You know you are not really going to have a full meal until you have paid more that two-fifty." To him, the whole sad story underlined the need to modernize funeral industry regulations.[2]

THE FUNERAL RULE

Despite recurrent critiques, for most of the twentieth century the funeral industry successfully fended off any form of regulation, except a requirement that funeral directors be licensed, which the industry welcomed, since it re-duced competition and provided members with the aura of professionalism. One editorial in an industry publication described the prospect of regulation in the stark terms of the Cold War, warning that "first among the American Institutions to be attacked are 'medical care' and 'disposal of the dead,' and if these fall, so may everything else that stands between the rights of the individual and the power of political and military authority."[3]

In 1963 Jessica Mitford's *The American Way of Death* renewed interest in government regulation of the industry, but it was not until the early 1970s that the U.S. Federal Trade Commission (FTC), charged with enforcing anti-trust laws, launched an inquiry into industry. The National Funeral Directors Association argued that the FTC had been spurred on by people who wanted to create a funeral-less (and doubtlessly a godless) society, but in 1975 the FTC concluded that

> it has reason to believe that bereaved buyers are in an especially vulnerable position and that their vulnerability has been exploited by undertakers through a variety of misrepresentations, improper sales techniques, nondisclosures of vital information and interferences with the market. Such practices have, the commission believes, inflicted substantial economic and emotional injuries on large number of consumers.[4]

The FTC established what has come to be known as the Funeral Rule, a key provision of which is the requirement that funeral providers post price lists. The days in which the price of the casket was the whole price of the funeral service were over. The rule also prohibited:

- embalming without permission
- bait-and-switch tactics
- impugning consumers who express concern over price
- misrepresenting public-health requirements
- refusing to furnish less expensive alternative forms of disposal, such as immediate disposition and cremation.

One industry supporter, Vanderlyn R. Pine, a funeral director turned sociologist, came up with the novel view that by protecting consumers, the FTC was placing them at psychological risk, telling *Business Week* magazine, "A service that is psychologically distressing but therapeutically beneficial might now be eliminated for price reasons. But the $50 saving that might result could cause hours on a psychologist's couch."[5]

While the industry was unable to block the Funeral Rule, it fought a strong rearguard action. As a result, the rule did not come into full effect until 1984. At the same time that it introduced the rule, the FTC, to underline the problems in the industry, ordered Texas-based SCI to return $150,000 in improper charges to consumers. These charges included markup on obituary notices and flowers and overcharging on cremations.[6] In 1994 the industry won an important victory when it had the rule amended to allow funeral directors to charge a non-refundable fee. It cannot be said that the rule had done much to protect consumers; including cemetery expenses, average funeral costs rose from $1000 in 1963 to $6000 in 1999 according to the National Funeral Directors Association.[7] Several industry commentators argued that by forcing funeral directors to go from a system where the casket constitutes the single price of the funeral to one where there is an itemized cost for each service from which the consumer can choose, funeral directors simply individualize each of their services and put a price on it. While the consumer might have more choice, the price is not going down.

In Canada the funeral sector is regulated at the provincial level (see Appendix for a list of provincial regulators). Over the years, most provinces have had separate statutes and regulations for funeral directors and cemetery owners. The insurance industry, which is involved when funeral insurance is sold, is regulated both provincially and federally. Some sectors of the industry, such as the manufacturers of memorials, are not regulated at all.

ONTARIO REFORMS ITS FUNERAL LAWS — VERY SLOWLY

Oddly enough, the anti-regulation Conservative government of Mike Harris in Ontario is responsible for one of the most sweeping pieces of funeral legislation, the omnibus *Funeral, Burial and Cremation Services Act* of 2002. The impetus for the changes came from the cemetery industry, which was look-ing for an end to a prohibition against cemeteries owning funeral homes. A number of cemeteries had already built visitation centres on their cemetery property and wanted to operate them as funeral homes. But to do away with the law prohibiting combined ownership of the funeral parlours and cemeteries, the funeral industry and the Harris government felt obliged to appoint a Bereavement Sector Advisory Committee (BSAC) in 2001 to review the industry. The Federation of Ontario Memorial Societies (FOOMS) was invited to provide informed consumer representation on the BSAC. It was represented by president of FOOMS Pearl Davie and Elly Elder of Toronto, who along with Davie was a member of the FOOMS legislation committee. The position of the federation was very clear — the prime responsibility of the Bereavement Services Advisory Committee was to the consumer and to enhance consumer protection in the deathcare sector. All components of the industry agreed to this approach. According to Davie,

> This made it difficult for the funeral industry to oppose the posi-
> tions that the memorial societies were taking. Everything we do in
> life boils down to ethics. What we try to do is approach it from the
> benefit of the consumer — and if it isn't ethical, it probably isn't
> going to benefit the consumer.

The Bereavement Sector Advisory Committee's mandate was to replace Ontario's *Cemeteries Act Revised 1991* and the *Funeral Directors and Establishments Act 1990* with a single piece of legislation. Davie believes it is a tribute to the work of retired judge George Adams, who facilitated the committee's work, that it was able to reach an agreement by the fall of 2002. Its report, which became the basis of the new Act, serves as an excellent list of what is wrong with the funeral industry. The report and the subsequent Act requires

- Full disclosure of ownership. On advertising, signs, contracts, and price lists, funeral homes will have to indicate whether they belong to a chain.
- A prohibition on "tied selling." Tied selling arrangements state that consumers can only get certain services or products if they buy other services as well. The committee said customers should be allowed to buy services on an à la carte basis.
- Standardized price lists. Currently companies are required to provide price lists to customers and the public, but the format varies among businesses — a standardized format will be required by the regulator to allow for easier comparisons by the consumer.
- Coverage of all sectors by a compensation fund, such as the *Funeral Directors and Establishments Act* Compensation Fund established in 1990.
- An end to obstacles to no-frill services. Under this rule, for example, funeral directors, would be required to handle a casket that was purchased elsewhere.
- A prohibition on high-pressure sales, misrepresentation and unconscionable consumer representations.

The committee also called for licensing of all salespeople, the introduction of an enforceable code of ethics and an industry-wide ban on unsolicited marketing. Suppliers would be prohibited from using information gained in a transaction to market other services. Davie has an endless list of funeral-home cold-calling stories. In her favourite, a funeral home in Alberta obtained a hospital's internal telephone numbers and began to phone patients in their rooms. "Imagine, lying in your hospital bed and getting a call from the undertaker," she scoffs.

The Ontario recommendations recognized the right of industry representatives to tell consumers interested in alternative methods of disposition and memorialization of their rights and obligations. If a consumer wished to scatter ashes in a park, it would be judged appropriate for the funeral director to remind them that the park might not always be used as a park and that, if it were used in another fashion, it would be impossible to recover scattered remains. While the new Act is supposed to increase the options available to consumers, this provision could give the green light to funeral directors and cemetery owners to try to talk people out of scattering their ashes. Davie believes that the industry's ultimate goal is to ban the scattering of ashes anywhere but in a licensed cemetery. She says, "the argument they always make is that if the land is not a licensed cemetery it could eventually be sold and used for something else, and you would not be able to dig up the ashes and move them." She thinks people are more comfortable with that prospect than the funeral industry appreciates. Adds Davie,

> I want my ashes to be scattered in Lake Huron, my husband wants his ashes to go over Niagara Falls. I do not expect Lake Huron to give back my ashes in the future. If a person is inclined to scatter in some place other than a licensed cemetery, then they often really do not care.

The Act also requires the licensing of bereavement counsellors, a new area into which funeral homes are branching. While the regulation is an improvement over the current situation, in which there are no standards or regulations for such counsellors, Davie remains troubled by the fact that most bereavement counsellors are affiliated with funeral homes. She says they all have the same idea of what a grieving person should and should not do. In particular, she says, they stress the importance of seeing the embalmed body and having an open-casket funeral. Davie continues:

> That is their idea of appropriate. My idea would be for everyone to visit me while I am alive, bring me flowers and then when I am dead remember what a character I was and have a party. I do not need a place for people to come and talk to me. I am not there. It seems to me a lot of this bereavement counselling has a bias for the funeral industry. They definitely keep in contact with the family in the hope of making a sale in the future. Every dollar they spend on the bereavement counsellor is money toward future business. I am sure the bereavement counsellors are excellent people and mean well. However, that is not necessarily the best thing for the grieving person, but it is a good thing for the business.

Many cemeteries require that customers buy certain goods, such as markers and vaults from them, arguing that this allows the cemeteries to control maintenance and upkeep costs. The *Funeral, Burial and Cremation Services Act* will allow this practice to continue, but will require the cemetery to sell these products at cost. Davie notes that the industry argues that it should be able to make money on something it is providing for the consumer. She adds, "if you are forbidding the consumer from buying something somewhere else, why should you be able to make money on it?"

A number of provisions in the Act protect smaller operations (although these recommendations also have implications for consumers). For example, there are prohibitions on:

- predatory pricing (selling at less than cost to discipline or eliminate a competitor)
- requiring a supplier to refrain from selling to a competitor
- having product specifications that are not compatible with other suppliers in the market (thereby making it impossible for consumers to buy products elsewhere for use in the cemetery).

The new Ontario Act represents an important step forward in the regulation of the deathcare industry. Although the Act received third reading in 2002, it has yet to be proclaimed. Since then it has already been amended several times. There is an admittedly lengthy process involved to implement the wide-ranging changes that the law involves. When I first interviewed Pearl Davie in the spring of 2006 she was on her way to yet another government meeting on the implementation process. Even her droll sense of humour could not disguise her frustration or her suspicion that the funeral industry was simply trying to grind the consumer representatives down. Says Davie, "Every few months there are pages and pages of proposed changes for me to review. On their own they are innocuous, but you have to make sure that they do not, when combined, frustrate our intentions." In the spring of 2007 it appeared that it would be at least a year before portions of the Act would begin to come into effect.

THE COMING BATTLE OVER SCATTERING

Where once a funeral director might discouragingly ask if you and your mother had not been getting along if you said you wanted to have her cremated, today's funeral director will not bat an eye at such a proposal. The industry has come to terms with cremation.

The next big battle will be over scattering, as funeral corporations campaign to limit the scattering of ashes to cemeteries. The first document I received when I visited an Arbor Group funeral home was a booklet on scattering. The woman who gave it to me said that it explained all the reasons I would not wish remains to be scattered. Even before I started reading, she continued, "Lots of people think that it is just dust that is being scattered, but it isn't, there are bones as well. This is why you shouldn't do it." The booklet's title is *Scattering: What you need to know before completing this irreversible act.* Its first page notes, "For some families this method of final disposition can be a meaningful experience that provides closure and a sense of inward peace." Wherever there is a "some," there is bound to be "for many" lurking close at hand. And the next line starts, "For many others however, Scattering can be a decision that ultimately leaves family and friends feeling a deeper sense of loss, or worse, feeling traumatized by the act itself." The booklet reminds readers, "Choices made under stressful conditions are often regretted later, when minds are clear." This is, of course, true of every other form of disposing of a human body.

The booklet lists the reasons for scattering, including honouring the deceased's request, simplicity, cost effectiveness or the belief that scattering is poetic. It then warns that

> At a time of heightened emotion, the *idea* of Scattering may become romanticized, but in reality psychologists have found that people often discover a need later on for an accessible and identifiable "place to go" as they come to terms with their grief in the months and years ahead.[8]

> *IMPORTANT: Please understand, that even if your loved one has made a Scattering Request, it is possible that he/she was not made aware of all the implications. It's worth thinking about. Please read on.*[9]

In other words, even if the deceased has made his or her wishes known, presumably not during a stressful situation, it is better in a time of stress to choose to ignore the request. As if that is not a choice you might regret for the rest of your life?

Much of the advice in the booklet amounts to common sense. If the ashes are to be emptied into the ground, there should be a shovel handy; you should give some thought as to what you are going to do with the container in which you carry the ashes to the scattering site; and you should think about what sort of ceremony you will have and who will lead it. There is a warning to consider the safety hazards, despite the fact that scattering ashes does not threaten anyone's health. Furthermore, the booklet cautions that seeing the ashes of a family member can be a shock, not matter how well prepared one might be. On further reflection, it is unlikely that the sight of these ashes is any more shocking than the sight of the embalmed body of a family member, but the funeral industry does not issue these sorts of warning about embalming or visitation.

In Britain, Sheffield University sociologist Jenny Hockey is leading a major research project into the ways that cremated remains are being disposed of in that country. Entitled *Where Have All The Ashes Gone: New Rituals of Mourning in the UK*, the project "aims to reveal the meaning and implications of private ash disposal and related materially-grounded practices, for both grief resolution and the provision of appropriate environments for disposal and memorialisation."[10] When asked to comment on the claims made in the cemetery's leaflet she wrote the following:

> Many of the people we interviewed had scattered outside conventional cemeteries (although many had returned ashes to other cemeteries or burial grounds, perhaps with a family history of burial there). They were happy with their choices but the key thing was establishing some kind of focus for grief — even though this did not need to be in a conventional burial ground. So we don't have any evidence of our own, or from anyone else, to support the argument that people regret scattering outside conventional sites — but the emphasis on a focus within our data does support the point that: "people often discover a need later on for an accessible and identifiable 'place to go' as they come to terms with their grief in the months and years ahead." The reservations interviewees expressed about conventional cemeteries were that they were impersonal, no other family members were disposed of there, they were vulnerable to vandalism. People talked about the dead becoming anonymous and lonely in such a place. This suggests that cemetery managers need to allow or discover ways in which bereaved people can personalise and give meaning to a collective site — which can of course be difficult since one family's personalising/memorialising practices and materials can offend a neighbour within a collective site.[11]

The decision to scatter or not is a purely personal one, with no significant body of evidence suggesting that there will be any long-term damage done to anyone if you do not scatter your ashes in a cemetery scattering ground.

REGULATION IN A SMALL PROVINCE

In Manitoba responsibility for regulating the funeral industry is scattered in at least four pieces of legislation (*The Embalmers and Funeral Directors Act, The Cemeteries Act, The Prearranged Funerals Act* and *The Public Health Act*). Authority for administering these Acts is also divided. *The Embalmers and Funeral Directors Act* establishes a Board of Administration to license and regulate embalmers and funeral directors and to prescribe courses of training and instruction. The board is chaired by a provincial civil servant and includes two funeral directors. It hears complaints from consumers — most of which reflect consumer dissatisfaction with price advertising — and attempts to mediate a resolution. Beyond that, there is little the board can do, other than lift a firm's license, which is for the most part too severe a punishment for the offenses that the board deals with. The board also does not publicize information about complaints, so if you are shopping around, you cannot call the board to find out which firms have been the subject of complaint.

In Manitoba there is also no requirement to list prices — and even when prices are advertised, they are not publicized in a uniform manner. For example, one Winnipeg funeral home advertises "immediate cremation, no service" at $650 plus taxes. This fee includes transporting the body (within a specific geographic limit), helping prepare the death notice, registering the death and preparing various applications, providing four statements of death, preparing the paperwork needed to authorize a cremation, preparing the body for cremation, the cremation and returning the ashes. However, the $650 does not include the cremation container. Since cremation containers are mandatory and at that home start at $175, the actual cost would be $825. Two other discount funeral homes in Winnipeg offer the same service at $800 and $890, but include a cremation container in their base price. In the absence of a clear regulation, funeral customers are doomed to find themselves comparing apples and oranges.

While the type of body snatching that nineteenth-century medical students engaged in is now a thing of the past, funeral homes have revived it in a new and highly competitive form. A Winnipeg friend of mine happened upon the practice when she arranged her father's funeral a few years ago. When her father died she set about phoning a number of funeral homes to determine which one would offer the level of service the family wanted at the most reasonable price. The first one that she called was one of Winnipeg's most well-known and long-established funeral homes and corporately owned. After getting their prices, she kept on with her research and eventually concluded that she wanted to deal with Voyage Funeral Home, a smaller low-cost funeral home. However, when Voyage attempted the pick up of her father's body from the St. Boniface General Hospital, it was told that the body had already been released to the corporate funeral home. Apparently, it sent for the body shortly after receiving my friend's initial call, even though she had not told them they were getting the contract. Furthermore, the hospital released the body in violation of its policy prohibiting such release without the authorization of the person responsible for the body. While the hospital was apologetic, my friend recalls that the funeral home was aggressive, claiming that it had been given the job and refusing to return the body to the hospital. In the end, it released the body to Voyage, which provided the family with the services it requested.

For the family, it became a bit of a joke: "We thought my dad would have had a big kick out of the corporation whisking him away and the small guy getting him the end. But if they had gone ahead and cremated him, it could have been devastating, particularly for some families at the price they charge." There is a lesson to be learned from this — if you are arranging a funeral and calling around for prices, never tell the funeral home where the body is. Hospitals are lax in enforcing rules regarding the release of bodies, and many people, overwhelmed by the emotions of the day, decide to let the funeral home that has possession of the body provide the service, even if it was not their first choice. In Manitoba, the provincial Board of Administration receives the occasional complaint about body snatching, but many people, including my friend, do not register complaints. They do not know that there is a regulator, they don't how to contact the regulator and, finally, having just gone through a death in the family and a funeral, they are unlikely to have the energy or interest to file a complaint.

In short, while significant improvements are in the process of being introduced in Ontario, in much of Canada the funeral industry is under-regulated and some sectors of the industry are all but unregulated. In many provinces there is still no requirement to provide a low-cost direct disposition, no requirement to list prices, let alone to list them in a standardized manner, and little regulation of the people who pre-sell cemetery plots and interment rights. The regulation that does exist is often fragmentary in nature while enforcement is spotty and complaint-driven.

The companies recognize that they are lightly regulated. Arbor Memorial Services notes that traditionally it has little trouble in passing the cost of any regulation on to consumers. While in some provinces it is required to receive regulatory approval for certain fees, usually related to interment rights, this process, according to Arbor Memorial Services, "has not had a significant impact on the Company's operations or significantly affected its ability to adjust prices promptly to match changes in costs."[12]

Preparing the kind of funeral plan outlined in the following pages can help your family members in a time of stress and may prevent them from being victimized. But there is also a need for provincial governments to develop regulations that reflect the dramatic changes and concentration that has taken place in the funeral industry in recent years and to put those changes in place before the Golden Age of death dawns on us in the coming decade.

PART TWO
FUNERAL PLANNING IN THE
AGE OF CORPORATE DEATHCARE

E VERY HUMAN DEATH GIVES RISE TO FOUR major questions:

- How will the body be disposed of?
- Will there be a service (either religious or secular) to honour the person who died?
- Will there be some form of permanent memorialization?
- How much will all of the above cost and how will it be paid for?

Creating a funeral plan essentially involves coming to terms with these questions. A funeral plan can brief or elaborate. It can address all four questions (and the many follow-up questions that can be grouped under each heading) or it can deal with a more limited number of questions. The next six chapters of this book provide the background information needed to create a funeral plan that addresses these questions. This information can also be used by someone who has the responsibility of arranging a funeral for someone else.

LET YOUR FAMILY KNOW WHAT YOU WANT

When it comes to making plans as to what you would like done to your body after death, there is probably no more important piece of advice than "talk to your family about your wishes." This is important for the simple reason that you cannot leave binding instructions for the disposition of your body. Unlike your possessions, your body will not become a part of your estate. Under Canadian law, a dead body is seen as a unique property, one that belongs to no one but the earth. Legally stated, there is no right of ownership of a dead body. The executor or administrator of a person's estate has the responsibility and sole power to oversee the proper disposition of the body, even if the will or some other document provides otherwise.

While you can use your will to name the person you wish to control the disposition of your body, bear in mind that the will might not be read until after your funeral. For these reasons, it is necessary not only to put your wishes in writing, but to discuss them with the individuals who will likely be responsible for arranging the disposition of your body. Unless they are comfortable with your wishes, they might not carry them out.

The fate of Sir Thomas Reddick, a former dean of the McGill University medical school underscores the risks of putting your funeral wishes in your will without also making sure family members are prepared to carry out your wishes. Six days after his burial in 1923, the executors of his estate read his will only to discover that Reddick wished to be cremated. When they dutifully went to court to have his body exhumed and cremated, his widow successfully challenged them.[1]

Even if family members are willing to carry out your wishes, it will be difficult for them to do so if you have not made your wishes known to them. So, whatever plans you make, share them. If there is no executor named in the will, the views of a spouse usually prevail — and if you are separated but not divorced, your separated spouse might have a stronger legal claim as to how your body should be disposed of than your current common-law spouse.

This section starts with a story about the work that a Winnipeg man undertook to assist people in developing funeral plans. The remaining chapters elaborate on the research he undertook outlining the role of funeral directors, organ and whole-body donation, disposition of the body and memorialization, a service to honour the dead and ways of financing a funeral.

CHAPTER 7

LITTLE NORM MEETS BIG DEATH

IN THE SPRING OF 2002 RETIRED WINNIPEG lawyer Norm Larsen took note that the Funeral Planning and Memorial Society of Manitoba (usually referred to simply as the Memorial Society) was soon to hold its annual meeting. Largely out of curiosity, Larsen, who had joined the society in the 1970s but had not been an active member for many years, decided to attend. Larsen's earliest exposure to the Memorial Society had been at meetings in Winnipeg's Unitarian Church, then located on Sargent Avenue, in the mid 1950s. Larsen describes the initial vision of the Memorial Society this way:

> The idea then was to promote simpler, cheaper, dignified funerals and to encourage people to think of what sort of memorial they wanted to leave. Did they want to go down with all flags flying with a $30,000 funeral or did they want to think things out, do something more modest and perhaps leave a better legacy to their family and to society?

When he showed up at the meeting in 2002, which was held at a funeral home in Winnipeg's North End, he found the society had not changed much in the intervening years. The society was, however, low on members willing to play a leadership role. When the executive director asked if anyone was willing to serve on the executive, from his seat at the back of the hall, Larsen could see everyone else stick his or her face into the afternoon's agenda in hopes of not drawing attention to themselves. Much of Larsen's life had been spent in various bureaucracies and he had vowed never to sit on another committee. Despite this, he put his hand up and asked how often the executive met, and got back the answer "twice a year."

"I wondered to myself how you could run an organization with only two meetings a year, but thought what harm could come of volunteering to serve as secretary," says Larsen. Shortly after Larsen joined the board, the executive director resigned due to a health problem, and the board soldiered on, taking much of its leadership from John Freeman, a retired United Church minister and former society president.

After a year on the board, Larsen, feeling that he did not know enough about the local funeral business to be able to make a contribution, resigned so he could educate himself about the industry. His first step was to read every book in the public library about the funeral industry. Then he started visiting funeral homes.

As he describes, his first visit took place by chance.

> I was out for a long walk that took me past the closest funeral home
> to my house. I went in and asked for a copy of the information
> they provided to the general public. They were very helpful. As I
> was looking through the documents I saw that they rented caskets
> that could be used at viewings and open-casket funerals prior to a
> cremation. I asked how much it would cost to rent such a casket;
> the answer was a thousand dollars. I was astounded, and the funeral
> director was surprised that I was astounded. I thought I was on to
> something.

Larsen always had a political and legal bias that favoured low-income
people. When he graduated from law school, which he attended after a brief
teaching career, he articled with Winnipeg lawyer Joe Zuken, a Communist
politician who was renowned for billing at Depression-era rates into the
1970s. Says Larsen, "The day I got my call to the bar, Joe offered me a partnership. I took it and immediately my income fell by half." After five years
with Zuken, Larsen spent seven years with Legal Aid Manitoba, and then
worked for both the University of Manitoba and the Manitoba Department
of Justice. Through all his experiences he retained an interest in what he
termed consumer law. And he suspected that when it could cost a thousand
dollars to rent a casket for half a day, the consumer might be at some risk.

His background as a lawyer left him with a mild degree of sympathy
for many funeral directors' unwillingness to quote fees. "It is difficult in law
to quote a fee because you do not know how long a case will take or how
complex it is going to be," says Larsen. He continues,

> Even the simplest thing can blow up in your face. One of the most
> complex matters I ever had was a real-estate transaction that I told
> the client would cost thirty-five dollars. For reasons that had nothing
> to do with me or the client, that simple matter became incredibly
> complex and time consuming, but I stuck to my quoted price.

Larsen also acknowledged that the work that funeral home employees
do is often very unpleasant. He says,

> They are often called upon to deal with terrible situations. It is not
> a job I would ever want to do. A funeral director has to be available
> twenty-four hours a day to take calls. It is a really tough business,
> particularly if they are picking up a body that has been dead for
> several days before it was discovered. It is hard to begrudge them
> some of this money.

Larsen's travels through the death industry were not without sobering moments. On a number of occasions funeral directors offered him the "grand tour," including a visit to the embalming room. Thinking to himself, in for a penny in for a pound, he said yes, but was almost overcome when he entered the first preparation room and was confronted with several dead bodies. Says Larsen,

> Death always takes me aback. Death, even when it is expected, it is a surprise. To see not just a body, but to see several bodies. "My God," I thought, "twenty-four hours ago, these people were all alive." But you can get used to it. I saw enough bodies on my travels to get used to it.

Over a six-month period Larsen met with funeral directors at twenty-one funeral homes in Winnipeg. "There were then twenty-two homes in Winnipeg, but I just ran out of gas. I could not make it to that last one," he says. He concluded that among the independent funeral homes there was only one that he would not trust to handle his own funeral. "Some of them regarded me with a certain amount of suspicion," he adds, "but I found them pretty friendly and generous in giving me information." His view of the corporate funeral homes was less charitable.

One of the benefits of membership in the Manitoba Memorial Society was the right to a low-cost immediate cremation and no-service (at the funeral home) disposition from any member of the Manitoba Funeral Services Association (MFSA). But as he went from funeral home to funeral home, Larsen discovered that many MFSA members did not know about this arrangement, while others said that they did not adhere to the deal. More distressing, he discovered that the Memorial Society rate was actually higher than some funeral homes offered for this service to people coming in off the street. "In other words," sighs Larsen, "the deal was no deal."

The next conclusion he came to was that prices were definitely negotiable in a funeral home. Larsen came across a description of what was known as the armchair test, which he describes like this:

> After going over the details of the funeral, the funeral director quotes the price to client, who is sitting in an armchair. The client hears it, heaves a sigh and puts his hands on the arms of the chair to ready himself to leave. The funeral director's goal is to keep you in the armchair, so he looks at the list and says, "Well, maybe we can massage this a bit." Before you know it, something is taken out and something else is added for free. The fact is that the funeral director does not want to let you leave without a deal. That's because for them each funeral is also a sales opportunity. Even if they only

break even on your funeral, it could bring one hundred people into the same funeral home, and the next time one of those people has to arrange a funeral they might well think of using their funeral home. That is one of the main determinants of where people decide to go when arranging a funeral — quite often people go to the last place where they attended a funeral.

In fact, one study done for the industry showed that when choosing a funeral home 47 percent of people simply select the home that had previously served their family.[1]

If funeral homes were willing to dicker, Larsen realized there was an even greater pressure to upsell, to encourage the client to buy more than they had originally intended to buy. Larsen adds, "The corporately owned funeral homes have much higher costs, therefore the pressure to upsell is that much stronger."

Out of his research, Larsen wrote two documents, a twenty-seven-page guide to creating your own funeral plan and a shorter document (reprinted in the back of this book) that constitutes the outline of a funeral plan. He also developed a presentation on funeral planning that he gives on a regularly basis to interested organizations. While it started out as a one-hour presentation, it kept getting longer and longer, mainly because people had so many questions. "If nothing else, my presentations provide at least two important pieces of information," says Larsen. "I got a handle on how funeral homes in Winnipeg are grouped — by that I mean which ones are corporately owned and which are independent. When I started I could not tell from looking in the Yellow Pages what was what. Nowadays they are a bit more upfront about corporate ownership." When Larsen was doing his research the Alderwoods Group (now owned by the Service Corporation International) had the largest corporate presence in Winnipeg, owning six funeral homes, three cemeteries and three crematories.

Secondly, Larsen categorized funerals into six basic approaches that combine the available options. Larsen's six types, with the price information that he discovered for Winnipeg in 2007, are as follows:

1. Immediate cremation (or "direct cremation" or "direct disposal"), with *no* service at the funeral home. This is usually the simplest and least expensive choice — *if* one buys only the basics covered by the fee. Prices range from about $650 to $2400.
2. Immediate cremation, followed by a memorial service at the funeral home. Starting prices range from about $1500 to $3000.
3. A funeral service (with the body present in a casket) followed by cremation. Starting prices range from about $3000 to $5000. This can be the

most expensive choice, partly because it includes the cost of both a casket and cremation. A casket can be purchased (and cremated with the body) or rented. The rental charge can be as much as $1000 — more than the purchase price of some caskets.

The next three options involve earth burial and have starting prices ranging from $2000 to $5000.

4. Immediate earth burial (or "direct burial" or "direct disposal"), with a graveside service.
5. Immediate earth burial, followed by a memorial service at the funeral home.
6. A "traditional" funeral service at a funeral home, with the body present in a casket, followed by earth burial.

After drafting his materials, he sent copies to all the funeral homes he had visited. An Alderwoods representative contacted him and wanted to know why he had ordered his funerals from cheapest to most expensive. Larsen responded by asking why the Alderwoods price list started at the most expensive and worked its way back to the cheapest.

While many budget funeral homes give out their prices, and the Alderwoods chain has a detailed price booklet, Larsen found many homes were unwilling to provide prices. The manager of one corporate funeral home responded that it was not necessary, saying "we only give our customers what they need?" "But how do they know what they want when they do not know what the choices are?" asks Larsen. When it came to getting prices, Larsen often felt as if he was pulling teeth.

The big corporations, which should be able to offer people all the advantages of economy of scale, were usually more expensive than the smaller homes. Part of the problem is that the big chains were created on the premise that the traditional funeral was here to stay. As Larsen says,

> They built all their profits into the casket and having the funeral in the funeral home's chapel. Now that cremation is taking over and people are holding memorial services in community halls, the profit in the casket is disappearing. They have to find other ways to make money. You get some of this bizarre business going on about urns such as picture frames, and porpoises in which some or all of the cremated remains can be deposited.

Larsen not only interviewed funeral directors, he also attended a number of funeral industry presentations. At one, he was told that embalming served to protect the public, a claim that contradicts current legislation. For instance, embalming is not legally required in Manitoba unless the body is transported within the province and will not reach its destination within seventy-two hours, a rare occurrence. Elsewhere he heard a funeral director say that the provincial Public Utilities Board approved the prices for prearranged funerals — a less than complete explanation of what the board actually does. Another home had a mandatory $245 stationary package in all its funerals (if you turned the thank-you cards, guest book and envelopes down, you were still required to pay $180).

While Larsen remains a member of the Memorial Society, he no longer plays a formal role in the organization — his publications state that they are "in support of the Funeral Planning and Memorial Society of Manitoba." I asked him if there was not a puritanical streak about what he was doing — after all, in Puritan Massachusetts in the 1720s there was a legal prohibition against "extraordinary expenses at funerals."[2] Reluctant to see himself as a puritan, he did acknowledge that some of the people he met at his presentations were obsessed with not being cheated. "They are so suspicious of the funeral industry that their main goal is to thwart them in terms of cost," says Larsen.

> I suggest to participants that the point is not to save as much money as you can or to thwart those awful funeral directors. The point is to have the kind of funeral you want. Figure out what you think you want, go to a funeral director and find how much it will cost and then determine if you are willing and able to pay that amount.

For these reasons he thinks funeral homes should be required to have à la carte price lists. "Right now," adds Larsen, "some homes offer you package deals, and if you say that you do not want the limousine or the stationery, there is no break in fees."

It is also difficult to buy many important supplies wholesale. The funeral director supply companies that Larsen contacted told him that they did not sell to the general public. As a result, anyone looking to buy a casket on their own would have to turn to place like LeClaire Brothers, a strip mall in west-end Winnipeg. From rural Manitoba, both the brothers, Reg and Aurele, have worked in the funeral industry for decades. Walking into their outlet is a little like coming into a carpet outlet, only instead of rows of carpet rolls, there are rows of caskets, each of which comes with a model name and sticker price. They say that their steel caskets sell for a thousand dollars less than what you would pay for a similar casket at a regular funeral home.

Larsen also struck up a friendship with Neil Bardal, whom he met through the Memorial Society. The two would lunch together on occasion, often over sandwiches in Bardal's office across the road from Winnipeg's Brookside Cemetery. Bardal would regale him with stories from the funeral trade's history and explain the ins and outs of casket selling in which he had been schooled. On other occasions they would reminisce about Larsen's late law partner Joe Zuken, who had gone to bat for Bardal at city council when the funeral industry tried to shoot down his efforts to set up a funeral home in a strip mall. Zuken pointed out that the worst that would happen would be that Bardal would go broke, which would be his problem, but if he succeeded, the city would collect an increase in business tax.

Larsen also says it was not uncommon for people to come to his seminars after paying far more than they expected to for a funeral:

> I think a lot of people say "I was astounded at the bill," but they pay. My impression is that there is very little formal complaining going on to the Board of Administration. In one case the family showed up for the funeral and was told there would not be any service until the bill was paid. The Board of Administration was appalled.

Larsen does not kid himself about the impact that he has had, although one funeral director told him that any funeral home in the city would be happy to give him a free funeral — and the sooner the better. Says Larsen, "The industry is very strong. They have seen critics come and go and it does not faze them. I did my first presentation in January 2003. It's 2007 now. I don't expect to do this forever. They can look at me and figure, 'he will not last, they never do.'"

Larsen is right. His personal battle with Big Death is rather one-sided. But the rest of this book is an effort to create a bit more of a lasting legacy of the work that he and Neil Bardal have done. It starts from the premise that, unless you are careful, you or your family can end up paying a lot more for a funeral and can also end up with a serious case of buyer's remorse. It does not take the position that all funeral directors are villains or thieves who are fattening themselves on public grief (in fact, many of the non-corporate funeral directors barely scrape by). It also reflects Larsen's belief that funeral directors perform many useful and valuable services. Unfortunately, driven by either corporate demands to fatten the bottom line or the difficulties that the smaller homes have, they also offer many pricey and potentially needless services.

CHAPTER 8

FUNERAL DIRECTORS
AN INTRODUCTION

WHAT CAN A FUNERAL DIRECTOR DO FOR YOU?

FUNERAL DIRECTORS HAVE EXPERIENCE AND skill in organizing and arranging funerals and funeral services. These talents are not to be taken lightly. Much of it can be difficult and stressful — any funeral director can talk about what it is like to go out to collect a body that has been discovered several days after death (in the trade, the term for collecting a body is a removal). A funeral director who is sympathetic to the needs and wishes of family members can relieve them of a great deal of anxiety and allow them to concentrate on those issues that are important to them. The basic tasks of a funeral director can be divided into three categories:

- Care and preparation of the dead. This can involve collecting the body, taking care of the paperwork involved in registering a death, embalming the body and preparing it for viewing, and then transporting the body to the site of the funeral service and then the site of final disposition.
- Conducting funerals. This can involve providing a site for visitation and a ceremony (either at the funeral parlour or offsite), providing a hearse, arranging for someone to preside over the service, arranging for pallbearers and attendants, and organizing a reception.
- Final disposition. This can involve interment, cremation and care of the crematory or cemetery.

Not all funeral directors provide all of these services, but it is not uncommon for them to arrange them all. While there are many criticisms that can be levelled about the marketing of funeral services, it would be a mistake to demonize the people who provide these services.

LICENSING AND EDUCATION

In Canada, provincial governments require that funeral directors be licensed. In Ontario, a person who wants to be a funeral director must complete both a program in funeral service education and a twelve-month apprenticeship. Ontario's Humber College offers a two-year program in funeral-service education. The first year is taken in class, the second is done by correspondence while the student is apprenticing. The first-year courses include Human

Anatomy and Physiology, Basic Microbiology, Embalming Lab, Embalming Theory, Orientation to Funeral Service, Moral and Ethical Issues in Health, Writing Skills for Health Sciences, Humanities, Pathology, Restorative Art, Issues in Grief and Bereavement for Funeral Service and Small Business Management. Following the apprenticeship, the student must pass three examinations. There are two classes of licence in Ontario, one that allows the holder to embalm corpses and fulfill all the duties of a funeral director and one that provides similar rights minus the right to embalm corpses.[1] In Manitoba, the provincial regulator grants funeral director and embalming licences to those who successfully complete a two-year course of instruction and training. Anyone can own and manage a funeral home as long as there is a licensed funeral director on staff. Additionally, in Manitoba, one does not need a licence to sell pre-need services. (Pre-need is the term for advance sales of funeral service. When someone is arranging a service after a death has taken place, they are at-need; if they are arranging a service in advance, they are pre-need.)

INDUSTRY TRENDS

Graduates cannot expect to get rich. In British Columbia, full-time embalmers and funeral directors earned an average income of $38,200 in 2000, at a time when the all-occupation average was $44,200.[2] In Saskatchewan in the same year, the average income for full-time funeral directors and embalmers was $41,110, higher than the provincial average of income of $35,461.[3]

Statistics Canada estimated that the average funeral involves approximately eighty hours of labour. The cost of that labour equaled 31 percent of a funeral home's revenues, while the cost of goods sold equaled 20 percent of revenue. Fees charged for services brought in 56 percent of revenue, while sales of merchandise accounted for 37 percent of revenue.[4] Products accounted for 20 percent of costs and brought in nearly 40 percent of revenue.

While funerals can be expensive, the funeral business is not necessarily as profitable as its critics sometimes allege. In Canada a funeral costs, on average, just below $500 in 1956, $500 in 1964, just over $1000 in 1972, $1500 in 1980, $2000 in 1984 and $3500 in 1991. Unfortunately, the federal government has not published more recent figures on funeral costs. Total funeral firm revenue in 1987 was $533 million; in 1992 this rose to $732 million. But as revenues rose, profit margins fell. In 1997 the fifty smallest funeral parlours in Canada had a profit margin of 1.3 percent while the fifty largest firms had an average profit margin of 10.1 percent. On the whole, profit margins fell from 15 percent in 1989 to 8 percent in 1995. It is not surprising that once they reached retirement age, the owners of family funeral homes often sold their businesses to large corporations. Increasingly, their children were unwilling or unable to take over an expensive low-profit operation. On the other hand, a business in a niche industry with, as everyone inevitably comments, a steady demand is unlikely to go bankrupt. From 1989 to 1997 only 4.9 percent of Canada's funeral homes ceased operating, a third of the national average for the same period. As one Statistics Canada report concluded, the industry was unaffected by the recession of the early 1990s.

Through the early 1990s there was an average of 1200 funeral firms in Canada, with an average of 10.5 employees. There were also approximately 3800 funeral directors, or about three per firm. In 1995, 81 percent of the funeral directors were male, 18 percent were over fifty-five years old, 6 percent had university degrees and 70 percent had post-secondary education. In 1989 there were 157 deaths per firm; by 1996 this number was up to 174. During the 1989 to 1996 period, the number of deaths in Canada increased by 11 percent, while spending on funerals increased by 18 percent.[5]

DO YOU HAVE TO USE A FUNERAL DIRECTOR?

While there is no legal requirement to use a funeral director, some government publications are misleading on this point. For example, the 2005 Government of Quebec publication *What to do in the event of death* states,

> As soon as a death occurs, contact a funeral director for burial, cremation or other funeral arrangements. The funeral director will provide all professional services related to the disposal of the remains and can handle all the formalities connected with the funeral.[6]

The funeral director can indeed do this — but there are other options, as a publication by the Ontario Board of Funeral Services makes clear. It states that you can use either a funeral home or a transfer service (sometimes called a removal service). A transfer service typically can pick up bodies, place them in containers (including caskets) and deliver the body to wherever the funeral service or interment is going to take place.[7] They can also deliver bodies to a crematory. In Ontario they can also specialize in immediate dispositions of the deceased (usually cremation). As no-frill operations, they do not do any preparation of the body or hold services, and, if you use one, you are likely going to find yourself having to do much more in the way of organizational work.

If you so choose, you can simply take charge of the body yourself. In such instances, you are a lay funeral director. There is no legal requirement to move the dead body by hearse or ambulance as long as the death did not arise from one of a number of specific contagious diseases. Aside from embalming, which must be carried out by a licensed embalmer, any person can legally make funeral arrangements for themselves or a family member or friend.

DEATH AND PAPERWORK

One of the key, and largely unnoticed, services a funeral director can provide is the processing of the paperwork associated with acquiring the permits that are needed to allow for either burial or cremation. The provincial vital statistics office usually issues these documents upon receipt of a medical certificate of death and a statement of death.

The medical certificate of death is supposed to be completed and submitted by the attending doctor to the appropriate officials within forty-eight hours of the death. This document outlines the cause of death. If the death takes place in suspicious circumstances or an autopsy is to be held, there could be a delay in the release of the certificate. While hospitals are not supposed to release bodies until this permit is issued, in many cases they do release the body on the understanding that nothing will be done to it until the certificate of death is completed.

The statement of death (or registration of death) provides biographical information on the deceased. While family members can fill out this straightforward form, in most cases the funeral director completes it with information provided by the family. The forms are not easy to obtain — for example, while a number of provinces explain the process on their websites, the forms are not available for downloading.

The following information may be needed to register a death:

Name
Address
Date of birth
Birthplace
Resident in community since
Citizenship
Date and place of marriage
Name of father
Birthplace of father
Maiden name of mother
Birthplace of mother
Names of children
Social insurance number
Occupation
Employer
Branch of military service
Location of military service
Serial number

When both the registration of death and the medical certificate of death are filed with the province, the province will issue a permit for either burial or cremation (in some cases additional coroner's permits are required for cremation).

Provincial governments will also, for a fee, issue what is known as a certified death certificate. This certificate is needed for financial dealings with banks, insurance companies or land-titles offices. Funeral directors normally supply their customers with a number of funeral director's statements of death as part of their fee. These certificates can be used to prove that someone has died when, for example, applying for special airfares to have a family member attend a funeral. One of the disadvantages of not using a funeral director is that it may be necessary to purchase additional certified death certificates from the government, usually at twenty-five dollars a piece.

THE STORY OF A LAY FUNERAL DIRECTOR

Deborah van der Goes, an Anglican cleric who lives in Nanaimo, British Columbia, along with her brother Jonathon and sister Theresa, organized the cremation of two family members without the assistance of a funeral home. She and her siblings fell into their first funeral directing experience in increments. In 1989 their father Philip died after a lengthy struggle with Parkinson's disease. While Deborah's mother Joan had been the primary caregiver, all three children had been involved in caring for their father and were nearby when he died. Days before their father's death, the children asked a neighbour to consider building a coffin for him. In the course of the conversation, the neighbour mentioned the very high fee that his family had been charged to transport their son to a local crematory. This piece of information served as the grain of sand around which their venture into funeral directing developed.

While the cost issue was the spur, of greater importance was the family members' desire not to become peripheral to the process. Van der Goes recalls, "we had been caring for our dad, with the help of home care, for so long, we did not want to be in the position of not having much to do of significance."

Their father died at home. He had requested that his brain be donated to the local hospital for research into the Parkinson's disease. On the trip to the hospital, Deborah and Jonathon rode in the ambulance, and she recalls that the driver recognized that the family wished not to be separated from the body. As a result, he stopped in front of the hospital, got a doctor to come out and certify the death, and then continued on to the morgue. "We realized that we were working as a team," says van der Goes. "It became less and less thinkable to hand the care over to the people who we were going to pay to take care of father." She began to arrange the cremation, only to be told by the crematory that they could not do so without involving a funeral home. Meanwhile her brother set about organizing the necessary paperwork. He too ran into roadblocks, mainly because he did not know the proper names of the forms he was looking for. He eventually contacted a coroner who was also a family friend. Deborah says the coroner understood the family's vision. She adds, "Soon my brother had the right forms, filled them out and was given the cremation permit. The crematory was still resistant, but the information that we received from the coroner gave us the confidence to insist we had the right to do this."

There had not been time for the family friends to build a coffin, so her brother began contacting local funeral homes to see if he could buy a cardboard cremation container. One turned him down flat, while another was very resistant, thinking that he was looking for a prop for a Halloween prank. When the home realized he was serious, the staff gave him one without charge. Deborah's husband, George, was recovering from surgery at the time, but managed to participate by composing the obituary. In a rented van they drove to the morgue, wrapped the body in a sheet, put it in the container, drove it home, wrapped it in ivy and drove to the crematory. Van der Goes does not recall what the family did at the crematory but says she looks back at the experience "with a huge amount of satisfaction. We were hammering out some pretty important principles for us. We had taken care of our dad so intensely, it just seemed so important to continue to do that."

There was still a dark cloud over the family, since Deborah's husband George was ill with what was to prove to be terminal cancer. At the time he told her that he would like the same sort of funeral that had been arranged for Deborah's father. The family eventually had to move to Toronto where, three years later, George died at home, in the family apartment in the Thorncliffe Park neighbourhood. In preparation, Deborah had found a company called Basic Funeral Alternatives, which was prepared to sell her a cremation container and provide the papers needed to register the death. "My brother arrived on the morning of the death," she says, "my sister arrived that evening. There we were again. My brother found his way around Toronto to get the necessary documents approved, and had far less trouble than he had before." The family had been supported by the Trinity Hospice Services and that support continued after the death, with the hospice team leader picking up the cremation container and taking it to the apartment.

The body was wrapped in a flannelette sheet, placed in the container and set on the hospital bed in the family living room. Starting that afternoon, family and friends gathered in the apartment and, following on the initiative of Deborah's five-year-old daughter Hilary, decorated the outside of the container with drawings and messages. Through the evening friends and people who had voluntarily helped care for George shared memories. When everyone left on that November night, the family moved the body out to the apartment balcony.

The next day the team leader showed up with his truck. The family took the container down in the elevator (which was set not to stop on any other floor) and the family set out for the crematory. When Deborah asked over the telephone that the family be allowed to be present when the body was placed in the retort, the manager told her that it was impossible since the space looked awful and there was only room for one or two people in the area. However, that morning the manager was not on site (an allergy to marble dust kept him away) and a young employee, after first sticking to the company policy, not only agreed to let the family be present when the body was placed in the retort but volunteered to lead the family in a brief motor procession to the delivery entrance of the building. Recalls can der Goes,

> It was lovely, with all the respect and flourish of a funeral. We were the ones who pulled the casket off the truck. Then we slid George's body in and at that point I simply read the prayers for the committal of the body for the fire.

As important as these experiences were for van der Goes, she thinks the stress should not be on doing away with the funeral director but on the family maintaining control of the process. She continues, "Families do not necessarily know what they want, but if they have the autonomy, they can discover what they want. We were able to make the decisions that were important to us; and I will be eternally grateful for that."

It is also worth noting that, in both cases, the deaths were not unexpected nor did the responsibility of organizing the funeral fall on the shoulders of a single family member — indeed, they received assistance from people outside in the family. Nor could the family have carried out all of the funeral preparations if there had been a desire to have either body embalmed (although it is possible to preserve a body for several days at home through the use of dry ice).[8] Taking on the role of lay funeral director can be a very important and fulfilling experience. It is a role that some people may have to take on for financial reasons, but it is not one to be taken on without considering all the tasks that must be carried out. A funeral plan should provide family members with guidance as to what should be done. It may make sense to leave them with some latitude as who actually puts the plan into effect.

CHAPTER 9

GIVING IT ALL AWAY
ORGANS, TISSUES AND
WHOLE-BODY DONATION

M ANY OF THE DECISIONS INVOLVED IN putting together a funeral plan
focus on what should be done with the body: whether it should be
embalmed, cremated, displayed, buried or scattered. But there is another
question to be considered: Do you wish to donate part of your body to a
person who is awaiting a medical transplant or do you wish to donate all of
your body to medical science, either for teaching or research?

ORGAN AND TISSUE DONATION

While skin grafting dates back several thousand years, and cornea transplants
were performed in the nineteenth century, organ and tissue transplants are
essentially a recent practice.[1] Contemporary transplant success rates are
very high, allowing people with failing organs to live healthy lives for many
years following the operations. It is now possible to transplant over twenty-
five organs along with tissue such as skin, cornea, bone, cartilage, valves
and veins.[2]

There is a large gap between the number of people who need organ
and tissue donations and the number of available donors. At the end of
2004, 4004 Canadians were awaiting organ transplants. During that year
1773 transplants were performed and 223 people died while waiting for a
transplant. The number of people on waiting lists has held steady at approximately 4000 since 2001. The figure of 1773 transplants (down from
the peak of 1882 in 2000) inflates the actual number of donors: in 2004
there were 414 deceased donors and 468 living kidney donors and liver
donors. The number of transplants exceeds the number of donors because
transplant teams are able to recover multiple organs from deceased donors.
The number of deceased organ donors in Canada has been level for at least
a decade. There were 437 in 1995 compared to the 414 in 2004. During
that time, the number of living donors increased from 230 to 468. (In most
cases, living donors are family members who donate a kidney or part of a
liver. Living donors can also donate bone marrow and the lobe of a lung.)

About 70 percent of the people on the waiting list are in need of a kidney
transplant. In 2004 there were 1044 kidney, 400 liver, 153 heart, 94 bilateral
lung, twenty-one single lung, twenty-six whole pancreas transplants and two

heart-lung transplants in Canada.[3] Canada's transplant system is effective: according to Health Canada, 98 percent of all kidney transplants, 90 percent of liver transplants and 85 percent of heart transplants are successful.[4] Donations are assigned on the basis of blood- and tissue-type matches first, then other factors are considered.

DECEASED DONORS

Across Canada, provincial governments and transplant programs have experimented with different ways to allow people to indicate their willingness to serve as non-living organ donors. Some provinces have donor cards that are distributed with provincial health cards or drivers' licences; others have registries. On a donor card, people can indicate how they are prepared to let the medical system make use of their body after death. In British Columbia, people can make their intentions known to a provincial registry. (See Appendix for a list of Canadian transplant programs.) Some people might choose not to fill out a card because they believe they are too old or too sick, worry that donors do not receive aggressive care, fear the process will prevent them from having an open-casket funeral or believe their religion is opposed to organ donation (very few religions take this position).

In reality, it is overall health at time of death rather than age that determines whether a person will make a successful organ donor, some of whom have been as old as ninety. While a person might be in generally poor health, they still might make a good tissue donor or cornea donor. In Canada, people usually become potential organ donors if they have been declared brain dead by two physicians who are not affiliated with the transplant program, a measure intended to ensure that organs are not harvested prematurely. While surgery is required to recover the organs that are to be transplanted, there is nothing about the process that would preclude an open-casket funeral. Anyone with concerns as to whether their faith condones such donations should speak with a leader from their religious community.

An article in the *Canadian Medical Association Journal* describes brain death as "the absence of all brain function demonstrated by profound coma, apnea and absence of all brain-stem reflexes."[5] The concept of brain death dates from the late 1960s. Prior to then, the signs of death were cessation of breathing and heartbeat, functions that can be maintained by machine even if a person is brain dead. Brain death does not include being in a persistent vegetative state (a condition in which there is spontaneous breathing, a measure of cardiovascular stability, and usually cycles of sleeping and waking). Manitoba's *Vital Statistics Act* states, "the death of a person takes place at the time at which irreversible cessation of all that person's brain function occurs."[6] To meet the criteria, all brain-stem reflexes (including, but not limited to, gag, cough, respiratory and corneal reflexes) must be absent when stimulated.

Certain motor responses must also be absent, and alternate causes of the lack of such responses, such as seizures, must be ruled out. Other causes of the lack of response, such as hypothermia and medication, must also be ruled out. It might take between two to twenty-four hours of observation to make an appropriate determination. Because is not always possible to make all determinations at the bedside, other diagnostic procedures might be required.

The concept of brain death is not without its critics, who point out that many people who are clearly alive depend on machines or devices (pacemakers for example).[7] Some transplant advocates have called for transplantation in the case of patients who could be described as being non-heart-beating donors (or having undergone cardiac death). These are individuals who are not brain dead, but are currently alive owing only to their being on a ventilator; their deaths would be triggered by the withdrawal of the ventilation technology.[8] Canada's critical-care physicians, who generally treat patients who would become transplant donors under such a scenario, have expressed reservations about the ethical implications of such a policy.[9] In 2006 Ontario hospitals carried out a limited number of transplants from cardiac-death donors, all initiated at the request of the family of the donor. While this practice might expand across the country, it remains a matter of ongoing debate.[10]

How to Become a Donor
If you wish to be an organ donor, it is important to fill out a donor card or to register with the appropriate provincial registry. Unless you have made your desire to be an organ donor clear to your family, there is a very good chance that, should you be rendered brain dead, you will not be accepted as a donor. In Canada, doctors will generally not proceed with organ donation without the consent of the next of kin (or whomever you authorize to act on your behalf in a living will).

Sybil Stokoloff of Transplant Manitoba points out that it is almost always an unexpected event that leads to brain death. "That is why it is so important for people to make their wishes known to their family. We ask you to carry a donor card, but we also need you to make sure you discuss your wishes with your family," says Stokoloff. According to Health Canada's website, family members will agree to an organ donation 96 percent of the time if they have been previously made aware of the person's wish to be a donor. This approval rate falls to 58 percent in those cases where the family have not been made aware of the person's intent.[11]

The fact that only a small number of Canadians ever fit the criteria to become an organ donor is in large measure a tribute to Canadian public-health measures. For example, seatbelt and helmet laws have reduced the number of accidents that lead to brain death, particularly in young people.

The fact that such injuries are not common makes it all the more important for people to make their desires clear to their families. In almost all cases, brain death follows an unanticipated incident such as a cerebral aneurysm or an accident that causes a head injury.

THE DONATION PROCESS

If you were to suffer such an unexpected event, and, after treatment in hospital, it was determined that it was not possible to save your life, you might become a potential organ donor. If you were thought to be a potential donor, attending physicians would contact a representative of your province's transplant program. Before your family is asked for its approval for a donation, two physicians not affiliated with the transplant program would have to declare you to be dead. If you met the various criteria to be a donor, and were in a major hospital or could be transferred to a major hospital, a representative of your province's transplant program would meet with your family. Together, they would review whatever information exists about your views on organ donation. Even if there were no signed donor card (or in those provinces with a provincial registry, no record of your desire to be an organ donor), your next of kin might still be asked to consent to organ donation. As can be imagined, family members are under tremendous stress in these situations. If you have made it clear whether or not you wish to be an organ donor, you will have made this experience slightly less painful.

If your family consents to organ donation, recipients are identified from local and national waiting lists, and surgical teams recover organs for transplantation. After the organ donation process is complete, tissues might be recovered. Unlike organs, tissue does not have to be used immediately. At this point, your body would be released to your next of kin who would then implement whatever plans you have made for your funeral. There is no charge to your family for having authorized the donation. The donation process is completely confidential; the recipient will not be told where the organ came from, and your family will not be given the identity of the recipient.

Many argue that Canada has one of the lowest donor rates in the industrial world. In 2004, the Canadian deceased-donor rate was 13 per million people.[12] In the previous year, the Spanish rate was 33.8 per million, the Belgian rate 24.4 and the Austrian rate 23.3. These countries not only have the highest deceased-donor rates, their organ donor laws operate on the principle of presumed consent: it is presumed that everyone consents to organ donation unless explicit instructions are left to the contrary.

In light of these figures, the question arises, should Canada introduce such a policy to address the gap between the number of donors and the number of people on waiting lists? Opponents of such a policy point out that the Spanish success is due to a number of factors, including, on the plus side, a highly effective system for identifying donors (the Catholic Church supports organ donation, and organ-procurement organizations are rewarded on a piece-rate basis) and, on the minus side, Spain has a higher percentage of motor-vehicle accidents than many other countries.[13] Canada has a far lower rate of death from motor vehicle accidents and from the sorts of cerebro-vascular diseases that lead to brain death. Many argue that the best way to increase donation rates is improved education among both health-care professionals, who might be reluctant to raise the subject with people who have just lost a loved one, and the public to allow for more donors to be identified and to ensure that those people who are comfortable with the idea of donation make their wishes clear to their families.

GETTING INTO MEDICAL SCHOOL

Agreeing to organ donation is, of course, no substitute for a funeral plan, since all organ and tissue transplant programs return the body to the family for final disposition. But organ donation is not the only way to keep on giving after death. Instead of burying or cremating your body, you can donate it to a teaching hospital, where it is most likely to be dissected by anatomy students or studied by dentistry students. (This is not the only use to which science can put your body. The American journalist Mary Roach examines the issue in surprisingly amusing detail in her book *Stiff: The Curious Lives of Human Cadavers*,[14] while another journalist, Annie Cheney, tells the more disturbing story of the sale of body parts in the United States in her *Body Brokers: Inside the Underground Trade in Human Remains*.[15] It is important to note that neither book deals with organs donated for transplant.) The supply of bodies for these purposes has a long and controversial history, both in Canada and Great Britain.

When a headless corpse was found floating in the Avon River in Stratford, Ontario, in the fall of 1876, locals suspected, correctly, that medical students, on the hunt for bodies to dissect, were to blame. An inquest concluded that the body belonged to Henry Derry, a vagrant who had died of tuberculosis in the county jail a few months earlier. Though a local doctor was questioned about two medical students from Toronto who had studied with him, the case remained unsolved until an embarrassed medical student admitted to the authorities that he had robbed the grave, cut off the head for dissecting and thrown the body in the river.[16]

This medical student was following in a long and grisly tradition. In eighteenth- and nineteenth-century Britain, grave robbing to supply anatomy students with cadavers was a booming business since the legal supply of cadavers, which consisted of the bodies of executed criminals, could not keep up with the demand created by medical schools. Some enterprising students financed their educations by working as nighttime resurrection men, as the grave robbers were ghoulishly called. The rise of body snatching was so alarming that it led relatives to place guards at graves for the first weeks following a burial. Graves were occasionally booby-trapped or covered with iron bars known as *mortsafes*. The fact that the common law held that there was no right of property in a dead body initially created problems in prosecuting early body snatchers. They couldn't be charged with theft, since if there is no owner, there can be no theft.[17]

In anticipation of the more baroque developments of the twentieth century, undertakers promised their clients the security of a wrought-iron coffin. Other, less scrupulous characters hurried the process along — and avoided the drudgery of digging their wares out of the ground — by selling anatomists the corpses of people they murdered. The industrious William Burke and William Hare killed and sold at least sixteen people in nine months in Edinburgh in 1827 and 1828.

Medical grave robbing was comparatively less common in Canada, but it did take place. In 1876, the year of the Stratford case mentioned above, Ontario medical schools were paying up to thirty dollars for a cadaver. The need for body snatching was reduced by the adoption of the *Anatomy Act* in 1843, which required that the bodies of those who died in institutions for the insane and infirm be handed over to medical schools. However, if the family objected — or the deceased had objected prior to death — the body would not be donated to science. Body snatching was more persistent in Quebec, particularly in Montreal, than in Ontario, since Quebec's public institutions were reluctant to follow the *Anatomy Act* requirements to turn bodies over to the hospitals. McGill University anatomy professor Frances Shepherd had to turn to grave robbers for all his cadavers — and often had to pay up to fifty dollars a body in the 1870s — a sign of Quebec's greater demand for surreptitiously acquired cadavers. He was occasionally charged and convicted of offences against decency and fined an additional fifty dollars. Shepherd's students were among the most energetic body snatchers and they frequently tobogganed their booty from the cemeteries on Mount Royal. When in 1875 a student was convicted of body snatching, his fellow students chipped in to pay the fine and paraded him on their shoulders through the streets, waving the tools that they used in their grave-robbing exploits.[18]

Today, universities rely almost solely on people to donate their bodies for further medical study. Most provincial governments have the authority to turn unclaimed bodies over to university medical schools, but very few bodies go unclaimed each year.

In some jurisdictions, people can either indicate on their organ donor card that they wish to donate their bodies to medical education or research or arrange a donation directly with a teaching hospital. For example, the University of Manitoba's Department of Human Anatomy and Cell Science provides, on request, an information package describing how to donate your body to the university. To meet the provisions of the Manitoba *Anatomy Act*, your next of kin (or person who will have a legal right to claim your body) has to fill out a waiver of claim, in triplicate, then have the signature witnessed. The university keeps two copies, while you retain one for your files. If the person who signs the waiver pre-deceases you, the waiver remains in effect. The University of Manitoba also provides a wallet card, showing that you have opted to donate your body to education and research. As an alternative, in Manitoba, you can simply check off one or both of the boxes on the donor card that comes with your Manitoba driver's licence to indicate that you wish to donate your body to research or education. In either case, when you die, the person responsible for disposition of your body must contact the university as soon as possible.

The University of Manitoba stresses that before donation, the body cannot be embalmed or subjected to an autopsy (medical schools embalm donated bodies, but they use a very different method than the one employed by funeral directors). The university might not accept the body and it will not necessarily pay all transportation charges. Nor will it accept bodies that have to be transported more than 322 kilometres (200 miles). Currently, the university subsidizes travel costs within that radius to the amount of sixty-five dollars.[19]

Practices differ from province to province. While the University of British Columbia accepts donations without a signed consent form, it prefers to have a signed form on file. Unlike the University of Manitoba, it does not offer wallet-sized body donor cards to potential donors. At the University of Calgary three forms have to be filled out, one of which is returned to the university.

There is a risk that the university will not accept your body. Factors that may lead to rejection include mutilation, excessive weight, extensive abdominal or pelvic surgery, extensive cancer or an infectious or contagious disease. The bodies of children and infants are not accepted — nor will the body be accepted if organs (other than eyes) have been harvested for transplantation.

Prior to dissection (which may not take place for several years after donation) the body undergoes medical embalming. Following the dissection and any other studies that may take place, the body is cremated. At that point, in Manitoba, your next of kin have two options: they can reclaim the ashes and dispose of them as they wish (in accordance with your wishes) or they can authorize that they be disposed of at the annual interment service the university holds at Winnipeg's Brookside Cemetery. If your family claims the ashes, it is responsible for all costs from that point on. The university's interment service is attended by staff, students, government officials and those family members of the deceased who choose to attend and is officiated over by clergy from the denominations to which the deceased belonged (unless there is a request for no religious service). The ashes are interred at the cemetery and, while there is a memorial commemorating all donors, there is no individual grave marker unless the family pays for it.[20]

One final point: for the most part, organ donation and donating your body to medical study are mutually exclusive. As noted above, medical schools will not accept a body that does not have all of its organs. However, you can include both options in your funeral plan. You can fill out your organ donor card (or register with your provincial agency to be an organ donor) and you can make arrangements to donate your body to your local medical school. If you do so, you are in effect saying that your preference is to be an organ donor if possible, but if that is not possible you would like to donate your body to medical education. Whatever you decide, the key step is to communicate your wishes to your family.

CHAPTER 10

BODY AND SOIL
FINAL DISPOSITION AND MEMORIALIZATION

For most Canadians, beyond donating one's body to science, there are three options for disposal of a dead body: earth burial, entombment in a mausoleum and cremation. This chapter examines each option, outlining the key questions that must be addressed in a funeral plan. Each of the three sections ends with a list of goods and services for which a funeral home or cemetery might charge in relation to the method of disposal under consideration. The text also lists price ranges for these services. The prices were gathered from funeral homes and cemeteries across the country in 2006 and 2007. It is important to realize that prices can vary dramatically from firm to firm and region to region. They are included to give the reader a sense of what these options can cost.

A fourth option for disposal, burial at sea, is not discussed. It requires a $2500 permit, which takes eight weeks to process. Since it is illegal to bury an embalmed body at sea, it is necessary to store the body in a refrigeration unit until the permit is granted. Also required are a special permit from a physician indicating that the body is free of contagious or infectious disease and a special, weighted coffin. Given these restrictions, burial at sea is a rarely used option.

EARTH BURIAL
Earth burial involves six major decisions:

- Will you be embalmed?
- Will there be a visitation?
- Where will you be buried?
- What will you be buried in?
- Will you have a grave liner or vault for your casket?
- How will your grave be marked?

Choosing earth burial can dramatically increase funeral costs, leading down a path that can involve embalming, purchasing an expensive casket, an expensive grave liner, an expensive cemetery plot and an expensive stone marker.

WILL YOU BE EMBALMED?

Embalming is usually optional. Each province has regulations about when or if it is required. A Quebec government publication states that "embalming is required for bodies exposed for more than 24 hours or whenever there is a delay of more than 18 hours before visitation."[1] The only Manitoba law relating to embalming is the *Diseases and Dead Bodies Regulation* under *The Public Health Act*, which requires embalming if a body it is to be transported within the province and will not reach its destination within seventy-two hours. But even then, the body does not have to be embalmed if it is shipped in an impervious, sealed coffin, or a less secure coffin if it is enclosed in an impervious, sealed container. An Alberta government document states that embalming is required if a body is to be shipped out of province. It goes on to say that "embalming is not usually legally required if burial or cremation takes place within 72 hours of death. It is important that the funeral home be advised if this choice is made, as it may take place automatically."[2] Similarly, the federal government's Office of Consumer Affairs warns that, "if you decide against embalming, inform the funeral home immediately. In most cases, except in Ontario, unless you give instructions to the contrary, funeral homes will usually go ahead with this procedure and charge you for it."[3] In short, embalming is *not* required, indeed it should be done only with the explicit direction of the family, but, unless it is explicitly rejected it, it could be forced on the family.

While embalming may be required if you are shipping a body to another jurisdiction, it is important to determine the legal requirements of the jurisdiction to which the body is being shipped before arranging for an embalming.

Two main — and related — arguments are made for embalming. The first is that family members (and others) can more easily come to terms with death if they are able to spend time with the deceased. This also allows them to create a picture memory of the deceased person. Family members and friends who have been out of touch with the deceased are able to say a final farewell.

Secondly, embalming makes it possible to present the body at a viewing and to hold the viewing several days after death. Without embalming, a viewing must be held quickly, before the body starts to decompose, although storage in a refrigeration unit (which most funeral homes have) or surrounding the body with dry ice will delay decomposition. People who chose this approach should be aware that the body will not resemble an embalmed corpse.

Until little more than one hundred years ago, almost nobody was embalmed and somehow the survivors soldiered on. On the other hand, we live in a far more mobile society and embalming provides opportunity for those who find solace in a final viewing. There are no right answers in these situations. My mother was very moved by the sight of my embalmed father; I was distressed.

Some funeral home representatives claim that embalming is needed to protect the public health, but until a body starts to decompose, it is no greater threat to the public health than a living body — probably even less so, since a dead body has stopped exhaling, excreting, sweating and wandering around and coming into contact with other human beings, which are the main ways that human bodies spread infections. In many jurisdictions embalming is forbidden if the deceased succumbed to certain communicable diseases. Embalming itself can be a health risk. In the 1990s the Manitoba government monitored thirty-six embalmings in eighteen funeral homes. The study found that in 83 percent of the cases, formaldehyde levels in the air exceeded international standards.[4]

Another final argument for embalming is the case of violent death, where family members have not been able to say a last farewell and the body is disfigured. In these cases, the embalmer's reconstructive skills might be able to create an image that is fit for viewing.

The process
Embalming is normally carried out in a specially ventilated room by a worker wearing protective gear, including a surgical suit, gloves and goggles. The overall goal of embalming is to slow the decomposition, a process in which enzymes and bacteria in the body begin to break down muscle and protein cells. Embalming fluids cause the protein to coagulate — thus slowing, but not ending, the decomposition process. The body is first cleansed with a germ-killing agent. This is followed by the arterial embalming, a process, in which embalming fluid is injected through the arteries while blood is drained through the veins. To embalm the body's cavities, a long, thin, hollow tool referred to as a trocar is used to pierce the various organs in the abdominal cavity. After gases and liquids are pumped out of the cavity through the trocar, preservative is pumped into the body

Embalming may require decisions on the following questions:

- Reconstruction of the body in the case of accidental death or death after long illness.
- Whether to buy clothing for the body from the funeral home or supply it from home.
- Hairdressing and makeup. Some people specify who they want to do their hair for their last formal appearance.
- The decoration of the viewing room. More specifically, determining what, if anything, will be on display in it.

through the trocar. These are the most invasive and dramatic elements in embalming. A hypodermic needle can be used to inject additional embalming fluid in areas where it is needed, while embalming liquids and gels can be spread on the skin's surface. In addition to the above, all the body's various orifices are cleaned, stuffed and in one way or another closed.[5]

WILL THERE BE A VISITATION OR VIEWING?

Embalming is often accompanied by either a viewing or a visitation in the days preceding the funeral service. While the words are used interchangeably, a visitation can involve simply an opportunity for the family to pay their respects before the funeral (often with the cremated remains present) while a viewing is an occasion for the family to view the casket, which is usually open. Funeral notices may employ such euphemisms as "friends may call" or "resting at" to announce a viewing. A decision to hold a viewing makes it more likely that embalming will be required. It may also involve the rental of a viewing casket if the body is to be cremated later. In the case of a full-body burial, one might wish to cut costs by renting a more expensive casket for the viewing and burying in a cheaper one.

Another alternative to a viewing, available in the case of home and hospital deaths, is for family members to simply request that they be allowed to sit with the body. There is nowhere else in the world you need to be at that moment.

WHERE WILL YOU BE BURIED?

Some people with strong links to the land still have the option of being buried in a private cemetery on the family homestead. For most of us, burial choices are limited to a cemetery operated by a religious organization, a municipality, a non-profit organization or a private corporation. Cemeteries are regulated by provincial laws that require them to be walled or fenced, that funerals be conducted in a "decent manner," and that the cemetery not pollute groundwater.

Telling Your Lot from Your Plot

Two terms regularly used in the cemetery trade are lot and plot. A lot is a single gravesite, usually four-feet wide by ten-feet long. A plot consists of a number of such gravesites, giving rise to the concept of the family plot. If you are going to buy a plot (or even a lot, in which you intend to have several people buried either as cremated remains or one on top of the other), it is important to clearly set out who has the right to determine who is going to be buried in it. Not all cemeteries distinguish between lots and plots, so it is worthwhile to have the cemetery representative explain what they mean by the terms. Also some cemeteries make a distinction between graves, which are reserved for markers set flush to the ground, and lots, which are for above-ground memorials.

Perpetual Care

Cemeteries are required by provincial law to establish a perpetual-care fund into which a certain portion of each year's sales must be deposited (some non-profit cemeteries may be exempted from this regulation, depending on the province). The amount that has to be set aside can range from as low as 5 percent to 40 percent depending on the jurisdiction. The amount collected for the perpetual-care fund often reflects the cost of upkeep of the lot. For example, a larger percentage of the cost is collected if the lot is located in a portion of the cemetery that allows above-ground markers, while a smaller percentage is collected for lawn cemetery lots where the marker is flush to the lawn (allowing the groundskeeper to simply run the lawnmower over the marker). Interest from the fund is supposed to be used to maintain the cemetery. It is a provincial government responsibility to ensure that these trust funds are properly managed and used appropriately. Although they are not required to do so under provincial legislation, Winnipeg's municipal cemeteries place 25 percent of the fee for a lot into a perpetual-care fund. When a cemetery quotes a price on a lot, you should find out if the price includes the contribution to the perpetual-care fund.

Double Depth

Everyone is familiar with the term six-feet under, but they might not realize that it is the bottom of the casket or coffin that rests at that depth. In Manitoba, for example, regulations require that the outer container be completely covered by earth to a depth of at least three feet. Graves that are dug to a depth of six feet create a covering of four feet. In some cases people are buried at a deeper level to make it possible, at a later date, to bury a second casket above the first casket. This practice, referred to as double occupancy or double-deep burial, is meant to save space and money. The first burial is more expensive because the excavation has to be deeper. In the case of full-size caskets, two caskets can be buried in the space usually reserved for one.

If you decide to go the double-depth route, it is important to realize that cemeteries will agree to place a second casket on top of an already buried casket only if the original casket is protected by a concrete burial vault (described in greater detail below). Without this protection, there is a risk that the digging equipment will break open the lid of the casket. The cost of the vault has to be balanced against the potential savings. Many cemeteries are no longer selling double-deep lots, citing health and safety problems in properly shoring up double-deep graves.

Interment Rights

In Canada, burial in a cemetery usually involves a real-estate transaction. You or your estate purchases a piece or property that comes with a document that deeds the land to your "heirs and assigns forever." This leads to an interesting question: who actually owns the land in most cemeteries these days? The cemetery owners can be spooked by this question, falling back on the position that there is no need to worry about who owns the land, since each plot can legally be used for only one purpose, the burial of a dead body. Many cemeteries now sell only interment rights as opposed to the lot. This gives the purchaser the right to determine who will be interred in the lot without ownership of the land.

Permanency

Price, aesthetics, tradition and convenience are likely to be the four main criteria on which people choose a cemetery and a cemetery plot. It is also worth considering permanency. For centuries, faith-based cemeteries seemed like good bets; everyone belonged to a local congregation and everyone ended up in the local cemetery. While it is clear that religion will be with us for a while yet, the future of specific churches and congregations is much less certain. The great population migrations from the countryside to the city has forced many rural churches with shrinking congregations to turn their cemeteries over to municipalities. Even in cities, many congregations are dwindling.

While private cemeteries say they sell "eternal peace of mind," which they say will be paid by their perpetual-care funds, there is no escaping the fact that corporations dominate the cemetery business and that a number of these corporations have experienced extreme financial uncertainty. Today's cutting-edge business could find itself consigned to tomorrow's ashcan; for one, witness the fate of the Loewen Group. In Winnipeg, for many years the privately owned Elmwood Cemetery was the final resting place for many of the city's elite citizens. But in the late 1990s it ran out of space. With no new lots to sell, the money in the perpetual-care fund could no longer cover the cost of maintaining the cemetery's picturesque riverbank location, and the property began to fall into disrepair. Eventually a private charity had to be established to oversee the cemetery's maintenance.

Towns and cities can disappear, but in many ways municipal and community-based non-profit cemeteries represent the safest bet in terms of longevity. They also serve an important price-setting function, since their prices often serve as a check on those set by private cemeteries. (Although in certain locations, private cemeteries may undercut non-profit cemeteries.) While many small towns have low fees for lots in their municipal cemeteries, they usually charge additional fees for anyone from outside the municipality. Many of the large non-profit cemeteries, such as Mount Royal in Montreal and the Mount Pleasant Group in Ontario, have been in operation for over a century.

WHAT WILL YOU BE BURIED IN?

Cemeteries are allowed to set their own rules for the sort of container a body must be buried in. Some do not require a casket, allowing burial in a shroud, which is a white sheet wound about the body. The body is lowered into the ground on a firm wooden board.

Most cemeteries allow homemade caskets as long as they conform to their regulations regarding size and shape. One can find plenty of designs on the Internet by searching for "how to build a coffin."

If you wish to buy a casket, your options are limited only by your budget, religious beliefs and aesthetic inclinations. The three major criteria for judging caskets are their appearance, permanence and the degree to which they can be personalized. In terms of construction, you can choose between metal, wood and cloth-covered wood.

Metal Caskets

The top-of-the-line metal caskets are usually made of bronze or copper, followed by stainless steel and steel. Steel caskets come in a range of gauges, usually from sixteen to twenty-two gauge (with sixteen being the heaviest and twenty-two the lightest), with or without a gasket (a seal that is intended to keep out liquids and gases). Those without a gasket are cheaper and usually of twenty-gauge steel. Copper or bronze caskets are sold not on their gauge, but on the weight of copper per square foot. A thirty-two-ounce copper or bronze casket is one in which the copper or bronze weighs thirty-two ounces per square foot.[6] In promoting its bronze caskets, the Batesville Casket Company claims that, "Many families choose bronze because it is superior to all other casket materials in strength, durability and naturally non-rusting qualities."[7] Despite all the high-tech developments, Batesville acknowledges that it does not claim "any of its caskets will completely prevent the entry of gravesite elements" or "preserve remains."[8] Any casket will eventually leak.

Wooden Caskets

Hardwood caskets are made of solid wood. Poplar and willow are among the least expensive, mahogany and black walnut at the high end. Veneer wood caskets are less expensive than solid wood caskets.[9]

Cloth-covered Caskets

Cloth-covered caskets are made from various forms of pressed board and particleboard. Do not be surprised if these are hard to find. On its website, Batesville states, "When budget is a challenge, cloth covered caskets are especially appropriate because they meet both the special needs of some families and Batesville's exacting standard of quality."[10] But you have to see a local dealer, because Batesville does not post any pictures of them.

I had read about how reluctant salespeople are to show the cheaper models, but I was not prepared for the straight-from-central-casting response I received from one corporate funeral-home representative when I asked how much a cloth-covered casket costs. Since no one ever buys one, she said, she was not completely sure where the price list for them was in her binder. Besides, she said, they were only pressed board.

Casket Linings

There is a wide range of casket linings — both coloured and patterned. The more expensive caskets have adjustable mattresses, which make it easier to pose the body for a viewing. Some casket companies sell full-colour inserts that can be fitted into the lid of the coffin for the viewing. These inserts could be a reproduction of the Last Supper, a landscape, a military insignia or a service club logo. The personalization comes with retractable drawers that can hold personal mementos, and can be left open at a viewing to encourage mourners to place keepsakes in them. Caskets can be customized by the purchase of special molded corners, featuring, for example, a pair of hands clasped in prayer.

Direct-sale Casket Dealers

It is now possible to buy caskets online and from discount casket companies. Before buying from a non-funeral home supplier, check to see if the funeral home will accept a casket purchased elsewhere. A representative of the LeClaire Brothers discount casket store in Winnipeg said that while funeral homes try to dissuade clients from bringing in an "outside" (and cheaper) casket, he has never known them to reject one. However, many funeral homes offer package deals on a range of services that do not include the casket if the customer buys the casket from their operation. While online casket companies have rush delivery, most appear to be based in the United States, meaning that delivery could be expensive and returns even more expensive.

In preparing a funeral plan, it is useful to visit local funeral homes and casket dealers to look at their products. Ask to see their least expensive models. If there is reluctance to deliver quickly on this score, you might want to think twice about dealing with this firm.

DO YOU NEED A GRAVE LINER OR VAULT FOR YOUR CASKET?

No matter how well built a casket or coffin is, the weight of the soil above it will eventually cause the lid to collapse. This can leave a sunken appearance at ground level and increase landscaping costs for cemetery. The cemetery-industry solution has been to require people to purchase either grave liners or casket vaults. These are the modern-day version of the mortsafes of the nineteenth century that were intended to keep grave robbers from making off with corpses.

Grave Liners
The cheaper option is the grave liner, which is a concrete box, slightly larger than a casket, placed in the bottom of the grave. The casket is lowered into it, and a concrete lid is fitted (but not sealed) over the casket.

Vaults
Vaults are much more ornate than a grave liner and at least double the price. They can be sealed or unsealed and — while they generally have a concrete core of steel — they come with a wide range of coatings. Vaults are intended to support the soil above them, provide protection against water entering the casket and can be hermetically sealed. A brochure for vaults made by Wilbert Funeral Services stresses the "peace of mind" that comes from the variety of "protection and personalization" options the company provides. The company offers everything from its "entry level" (making it sound as if death were a career move) Monticello vault to its triple-reinforced Wilbert Bronze. The pink Cameo Rose is "an exquisite choice for those desiring a feminine vault." The Bronze Triune (the name is meant to conjure up the idea of three-in-one protection) features "accent bars and special emblems" and comes with:

- Triple-reinforcement with bronze, a high-impact ABS Trilon® thermo-plastic interior, and an ABS Marbelon™-encased plastic exterior Brass Memorialization Plus™ capsule
- Solid die-cast handles and personalized bronze nameplate
- Brilliant carapace finished with non-rusting bronze
- Ultra high-strength concrete core.

With its durable concrete exterior and a cover and base lined with bronze and high-impact ABS Trilon® thermoplastic, it sounds as if the Bronze Triune is ready to be blasted into space rather than stuck in the ground for eternity.

You can personalize your vault (as if placing your mortal remains in them is not personalization enough). A scroll (which identifies the location of the local vault manufacturer) and personal messages, all providing "a way to record final thoughts or memories," can be inserted into a brass capsule in most of the vaults.[11]

Some cemeteries require vaults or liners to prevent the ground from sinking in over the graves. A vault salesperson also stressed to me that family members are likely to be distressed when they come back to visit a grave and see that the earth above it has collapsed. Another argument for vaults is that they protect one's investment in an expensive casket — and the better quality the vault, the better the protection. The price that one pays for a casket is not an investment, it is an expense. By purchasing a modestly priced casket, there is little reason to purchase an expensive protective vault, since there is less of an "investment" to protect.

A high-quality vault with a personalized capsule will make it possible for the authorities to determine who is buried in the vault if some natural disaster such as a flood should ever wash your vault and casket away. This can happen, but these events are rare, and one could probably find a more satisfying way to spend $3000. In the end, remember no matter how many times the casket companies use words like vault and protection, eternal protection of a dead body is impossible.

HOW WILL YOUR GRAVE BE MARKED?

Options for marking a grave will be determined in part by the choice of cemetery. Many cemeteries do not require that any form of memorial be placed at the burial site. In lawn cemeteries (sometimes called memorial gardens) markers or plaques (usually made of granite or bronze) must be flush to the ground; tombstones, monuments and fenced-in family plots are forbidden. Cemeteries also set rules as to the types of materials that can be used. Wood and concrete are often forbidden. Rules govern borders, fences, walls, flowers, hanging baskets and wreaths. Newer forms of memorialization include benches, rocks and even birdbaths, often with pictures or sentiments engraved on them.

There is usually a separate cost for the marker or monument and the base (in the case of a monument, an in-ground concrete foundation is also required) and for installing them. While some funeral homes and all cemeteries sell markers, you can also buy them from private memorial companies. Some cemeteries require that the marker be purchased from them, while others charge a higher installation fee for markers that are purchased from outside suppliers.

Virtual Memorialization

Beyond the cemetery, a whole new world of virtual memorialization has developed, ranging from official sites such as Canada's virtual war memorial, which allows one to search information on 116,000 people who lost their lives in military service, to commercial web pages that will post eternal notices about you and your life.

According to the *New York Times*, one of the problems plaguing Internet memorial sites are people who have no compunction about posting ill of the dead. One of the largest of these sites, Legacy.com, claims that it carries obituary notices for most people who die in the United States each year. U.S. newspapers fund the site to publish each death notice for a limited time. Mourners can choose to pay to keep the notice up longer. The site allows people to post messages on its guest books and over half of Legacy's seventy-five employees spend their time guarding against inappropriate messages.

Examples of the sorts of messages that have been blocked include those from embittered children such as, "Reading the obit, he sounds like he was a great father. His son, Peter." Others relive conflicts from the past: "I sincerely hope the Lord has more mercy on him than he had on me during my years reporting to him at the Welfare Department."[12]

A number of funeral homes now produce brief videos biographies for broadcast at memorial services. For a fee, some companies will also make the videos available on their websites.[13]

WHAT ARE THE COSTS ASSOCIATED WITH BURIAL?

The following prices are meant to provide a starting point for investigating the cost of preparing your funeral. Some funeral homes combine some of these costs in packages, while others charge a separate fee for each. It is important to recognize that most of the services listed below are optional. In earth burial, for example, it is perfectly acceptable to forego a coffin and be buried in a shroud. At the same time, it important to recognize that certain decisions lead to additional costs. A viewing will require a casket (either rented or purchased), earth burial is likely to require transportation to the cemetery and the purchase of a cemetery lot does not cover the cost of digging the grave or filling it in (or as it is termed in the industry, "opening and closing"). You may hear people in the funeral industry speak of cemetery services; they are not talking about a service held at a cemetery, but are referring to the opening and closing of a grave, crypt or niche, placing the vault, setting the marker and maintenance.

Potential Earth Burial Costs

Funeral-home Costs
- Embalming: $300 to $600.
- Sanitation: Dressing, casketing and cosmetology: $125 to $165.
- Viewing/visitation: $124 to $325. These fees are higher on weekends and in the evening.
- Casket: Prices can start as low as $600 to $700 and go up to $12,000 for a bronze casket.
- Transportation costs: $220 to remove and transport the body to the funeral home within a fifty-kilometre radius.
- Vehicles: One Winnipeg funeral home charges $165 for the hearse, which carries the funeral director and the minister, $125 for the limousine for family and $225 for a second limousine. One corporate home charges $230 to transport a body to a cemetery, $230 to transport the family, $170 to transport flowers or equipment and $170 to transport clergy or pallbearers.

Cemetery Costs

- Cemetery lot. If you are buying in a municipal cemetery and you do not live in the municipality, expect to pay a non-residency fee. In 2006, a Winnipeg cemetery charged $1055 for a single lot, $120 for a lot for an infant up to two years of age and $445 for a child from two to ten years of age. A British Columbia cemetery charged between $1455 to $2455 for lots.
- Perpetual-care fund: This depends on cost of the lot.
- Pallbearers: Between $25 to $35 each if provided by funeral home.
- Opening and closing the grave: These costs vary on the time of year and depth of the grave. To be buried at four feet in one Winnipeg cemetery costs $275. It will cost $650 for single depth and $995 for double depth during summer and fall, and $725 or $1065 for these depths during winter and early spring. There are additional charges for services held late in the day or on weekends.
- A vault or grave liner: $295 to $20,695.

Memorial Costs

- Installation of vault or grave liner: $100.
- Headstone or marker: Flat grave markers (brass or marble) start at about $400 but modest bronze markers can run close to $1000, upright tombstones at about $700.
- A base for the headstone or marker: $300.
- Installation of the headstone or marker: Starting at $140, rising depending complexity of installation.

In addition, many funeral homes now charge a basic service fee (which used to be built into the cost of the casket). This is intended to cover the services of the funeral director, the staff and overhead. At one corporate funeral home this amount is $1275 (the company also offers a number of, what it terms, "minimal service funerals," for which the service fee is $900). This does not include the fee the funeral home charges if it arranges the funeral service.

Cemeteries may also charge administrative fees and additional fees for such services as the provision of tents and artificial grass at the gravesite.

ENTOMBMENT IN A MAUSOLEUM

A mausoleum is an above-ground tomb, a name derived from King Mausolus's tomb in Halicarnassus in Asia Minor, a structure so opulent it was one of the wonders of the ancient world. For most of history, mausoleums have been relatively private affairs, built by the rich for themselves or their families.

These are the stone and mortar buildings decorated with chains and locks, such as those that figured with great regularity in the television program *Buffy the Vampire Slayer*. In more recent times we have seen the development of multi-story mausoleums in private cemeteries. Rather than burying bodies underground, they are entombed (the terms immured or interred are used to described the process) in separate compartments called crypts. Crypts were originally rooms or vaults built beneath churches that were used as burial places. Contemporary crypts are concrete chambers, often in multi-story buildings. After the body is entombed, the crypt is sealed behind a panel that faces into a common area. A memorial plaque is usually placed on the outside of the panel.

While the cost of building a mausoleum can be high, from the cemetery's point of view it is a very efficient use of space. The cemetery can dispose of more bodies in a smaller space than in a traditional graveyard, need not worry about the cost of grave digging or cutting the grass and is relieved of the landscaping work involved in filling in collapsed graves. Since most mausoleums are indoors, visitors do not have to brave the elements to visit. But it is generally more expensive than either earth burial or cremation.

The mausoleum is another real estate market. The crypts at eye level and inside are usually the most expensive, the ones at ground level are cheaper and those on the outside of the building the cheapest. To cut costs there are numerous ways to place more than one casket in a mausoleum crypt: end-to-end, side by side and the Westminster (named after the British practice of burying significant people in the floor and basement of Westminster Abbey, in which one casket is entombed below floor level and the second casket above it).

Entombment means protection from the elements. But it also means that your body is a threat to the mausoleum. There is a rich if distressing literature on the problems that have occurred when bodies liquefy and leak out of the caskets. As a result, there is often a requirement that entombed bodies be embalmed and placed in sealed metal caskets.

With a few variations, one can expect many of the same sorts of costs listed above in relation to earth burial. For example, one will have to pay for a casket (an expensive one that can be hermetically sealed), transportation, vehicles, pallbearers, some form of memorial to be placed on the crypt (often in the $700 range), entombment ($600), the placement the memorial on the crypt ($125) and, in all likelihood, embalming ($300 to $600). The big difference comes in the cost of the crypt. While crypts on the outside walls of mausoleums can be had in the $5000 range, interior crypts run from $9600 to $14,000 for a single crypt and from $13,000 to $28,000 for a double crypt. There is also a significant contribution to the perpetual-care fund. One can also expect to be charged a variety of service fees by the funeral home.

CREMATION

Cremation is now the most common form of disposition of a body in Canada. According to the Cremation Association of North America, in 1996, 39.5 percent of Canadian deaths resulted in cremation, a figure that had risen to 56 percent in 2004, with 2003 being the year the figure crossed the 50 percent mark. British Columbians were the most likely to cremate, while residents of Nunavut the least likely.[14]

Before cremation, crematory staff remove all metals along with any pacemaking device, which would explode in the heat. The body is then placed in a rigid container made of cardboard or wood and slid into a large gas-fired furnace called a retort. Cremation containers are not required by law, but are required by all crematories. Crematories set their own standards for the sort of container they will allow to be used in cremations. This serves to meet environmental standards and allows some crematories to increase revenues.

The heat in a retort, which can reach between 760 to 1150° C, evaporates the liquid in the body while the flames, which usually come down from above, incinerate the flesh and the container. The process usually takes from one to three hours, and can consume twenty litres of natural gas.[15] At the end of the process, all that remains are crumbled bones. After the cremation is completed, the remains are raked out of the retort and taken to a workstation where prosthetics such as artificial joints are removed and a magnet is passed over the remains to remove any small metal pieces. The remains that do not pass through a fine wire mesh are placed in a mill, known as a cremulator, and ground into ash. Weighing no more than two to three kilograms, the ashes are usually placed in a clear plastic bag.

If you choose cremation there are three questions to consider:

• What do you wish to happen before cremation?
• Where to you wish to be cremated?
• What do you wish done with your ashes?

WHAT DO YOU WISH TO HAPPEN BEFORE CREMATION?

For decades funeral directors vigourously opposed cremation because they believed that it ruled out the possibility of embalming and the sale of an expensive container for the memorialization of the remains.

In reality, there is nothing about cremation that precludes a traditional viewing and a funeral with the body present in a casket, although all this results in a more expensive funeral. At one funeral home, I was told that for a pre-cremation viewing I could rent a casket for $950, but would also have to pay an additional $915 for a special liner for the casket. The liner is not a rental — as the representative told me, "Once you go into that liner, you are not coming out." One can chose "direct cremation," which means that there will be no embalming and no viewing, or opt for embalming and viewing before cremation. The later choice requires addressing the questions raised in the earth burial section of this chapter that deal with embalming and viewing.

WHERE DO YOU WISH TO BE CREMATED?

While virtually all funeral homes will arrange a cremation, not all funeral homes have their own crematory. Those without one simply contract out their cremations to funeral homes that have crematories.

When choosing a crematory, you might wish to consider the following questions:

- Can family member or a friend supervise the cremation and be with the body while it is cremated? And will the funeral home charge an additional fee for this?
- Where will the body being taken for cremation?
- Are they licensed? This may sound silly, but the U.S. crematory that was stashing bodies in the back lot was not licensed.
- Do they empty the retort after every use?
- What type of sorting process is used after the body is cremated?
- How will the cremated remains be returned to you?

WHAT DO YOU WISH DONE WITH YOUR ASHES?

Cremation constitutes the final disposition of a human body. In other words, when family members pick up the package of ground-up ashes (or, as they are often called in the funeral industry, the cremains), from the funeral director, they are under no legal obligation to do anything further with them. While they can pay to have them buried in a cemetery or scattered in a cemetery's scattering ground, they can also put them on the shelf in a bedroom closet, where a friend of mine has kept her parents for years, or scatter them in a wide range of other locations at no cost.

Some people never even bother to collect the ashes from the crematory. In these cases, it is common for the crematory to keep the ashes for a year and then inter them in a common scattering ground. At the other end of the spectrum, ashes can be blasted into space as was done with LSD advocate Timothy Leary and *Star Trek* creator Gene Rodenberry. In some places it is possible to arrange to have the carbon given off in the cremation process collected and made into a diamond. These are all pricey options; for most of us the real options are:

- scattering
- preservation in an urn

- burial in the earth
- inurnment in a columbarium
- memorialization in a structure in a cemetery other than a columbarium

Scattering

If you wish to have your ashes scattered, you should make this very clear to your family members since, under certain circumstances, they might come under heavy pressure to have them interred.

The key limitation on scattering is that one cannot scatter ashes — or anything else — on private property without the owner's permission. On the issue of scattering on public property, a number of government publications each have something slightly different to say. The federal Office of Consumer Affairs states that cremated remains "are pure and represent no health risk. You're free to take care of the ashes as you see fit."[16] The Government of Quebec's publication *What to do in the event of death* states,

> No law indicates the manner in which the ashes of the deceased must be disposed of. They can therefore be disposed of anywhere according to the wishes of the deceased or the succession, provided they are disposed of in keeping with public order.[17]

An Alberta government publication says,

> Scattering of remains is usually permitted on Crown and publicly owned lands. Permission must be obtained ahead of time in all cases. In national parks (e.g., Banff, Jasper), scattering cremated remains in water is prohibited, but remains can be "cast to the wind." In provincial parks, forests and wilderness areas (e.g., Kananaskis), scattering is allowed anywhere, but permission is required to scatter remains over lakes and rivers.[18]

The Ontario Board of Funeral Services' funeral planning guidebook states that aside from scattering on your own property or in the designated scattering ground of a cemetery, you can scatter on private property with the owner's consent and you may "scatter the cremated remains on Crown Land without consent."[19]

While most private cemeteries would rather not see scattering take place at all, they certainly wish to see it restricted to their scattering grounds and they never forget to remind people that scattering is an irreversible process.

Preservation in an Urn

Because cremated remains represent no health risk, there is no need for a special container. An urn is simply a container into which one places cremated human remains. It is doubtful that there is a home in Canada that does not have a container that could serve as an urn. It is also the case that just about every container that can be used to hold human remains, from golf bags to lunch boxes, has probably been used somewhere. However, many funeral homes seek to replace the revenues that they have lost owing to the decline of the traditional funeral through the sale of urns and other memorialization paraphernalia.

Jessica Mitford looked forward to the day when cremation might usher in a world of funerals without fins. Instead, the casket companies are outdoing each other to give urns fins — literally, in the case of the many dolphin-shaped urns. The following is a listing of the various names of the urn lines produced by the Batesville Casket Company: Cast Bronze, Cast Acrylic, Cloisonné, Nambé, The Garden Series (which features birdbaths and pedestals), The Scattering Series, Infant & Youth, Sheet Bronze, Hardwood and Solid Marble. And that is only the beginning. There are also lockets into which a portion of the deceased's ashes can be poured. Or ashes can be placed in a picture frame containing a photograph of the deceased. Memorialization represents the supersizing of cremation, adding endless product lines to a process that was once associated with simplicity.

When Winnipeg potter JoAnna Lange was helping to arrange for her great uncle's funeral she was appalled by the cost. Looking back on it, she says, "I thought it was reprehensible. People are so vulnerable and the costs are so high." She knew from her own work that there was nothing special about the mass-produced urns that funeral homes were selling for upwards of $400. At the time she had no urns in stock, and it would have taken her several weeks to create and fire one, but since then she has produced a number of urns for friends, selling them for seventy-five dollars. She points out that even if you do not have the time to have an urn custom-made, many pottery galleries sell pots that would make serviceable and attractive urns for reasonable prices. There are other, creative ways, to combine pottery, ashes and memorialization. She knows of a number of cases where potters were asked to work the ashes of the deceased (often a potter) into the clay from which a pot or a number of pots have been created. At these times, she says, "friends and family gather round the kiln for a ceremonial firing." According to Lange, "There are lots of creative options and most potters would be very honoured to assist."

Burial in the Earth
Aside from blasting them into space, earth burial is one of the most expensive ways of disposing of cremated remains. The one advantage over more traditional earth burial is that it is possible to bury three or four urns in one lot. The City of Winnipeg allows the interment of one body and three cremated

remains or four cremated remains and no body in a traditional earth burial lot. It also sells cremation lots that hold two sets of cremated remains. The cemeteries that require vaults for earth burial also require vaults for earth burial of ashes.

Wilbert Funeral Services offers mini versions of its full-size vaults for urns. Just because you are being cremated does not mean you have to deprive yourself of the thrill of having your remains protected by a Bronze Triune or a Cameo Rose, each of which sells in the thousand-dollar range.

Inurnment in a Columbarium

Urns can be placed in a niche in a columbarium, the cremation version of entombment in a mausoleum. Columbarium comes from the Roman word for dove, and was inspired by "dovecotes" — shelters with nestholes for domesticated birds. In ancient Rome, jars of cremated remains were placed in niches in underground vaults. Today a columbarium is essentially any structure with separate niches for cremated human remains.

Today, there are both indoor and outdoor columbariums. Indoor columbariums are large, above-ground buildings, the walls of which are usually lined with locked glass cases. The cases are divided into niches, each of which can hold one urn, as well as mementos and personal keepsakes. As with mausoleums, the most expensive niches are at eye level. Outdoor columbariums are usually stone structures, often with granite fronts, about five- or six-feet high, with three to four rows of niches. There are numerous designs, including circular and spoked. Each niche can usually hold a number of containers of cremated remains. In some cases, memorial information can be engraved into the stone or on a plaque that is attached to the wall.

Memorialization in a Structure in a Cemetery

Cemeteries have developed many novel types of memorialization. These take the rather conventional (and useful and admirable) approach of having a memorial bench placed in a public park to a far more commercial level. For example, cemeteries now sell memorial benches that doubles as urns. Touted as being crafted from the "finest granite and polished to a rich lustre" they look very uncomfortable.[20]

At Winnipeg's municipally owned Brookside Cemetery there is a communal ash crypt that was established at the behest of the Memorial Society in 1977. For $215, one can have an urn lowered into a subsurface crypt; the urn remains in the crypt and the ashes remain in the urn.

An increasing number of cemeteries have ossuaries into which cremated remains can be deposited. This can be one of the least expensive ways of disposing of cremated remains. Where, in the past, ossuaries were depositories for the bones of the dead (often after they had been dug up from the churchyard), contemporary ossuaries are underground vaults, usually of pre-cast concrete, intended to hold the ashes of those who have been cremated. At the surface level, there is usually a stone structure that can serve as site for a graveside ceremony. In a lectern or column in this structure there is usually an opening into a chute that descends into the ossuary. After a ceremony, the ashes are deposited through the opening into the ossuary where they commingle with previously deposited ashes. Cemeteries with ossuaries often have large memorials, shaped like an open book, onto which memorial plaques can be placed.[21]

HOW MUCH MIGHT YOU EXPECT TO PAY FOR A CREMATION?

As noted above, cremation constitutes final disposition of a body. Therefore many of the usual costs associated with funerals and burial are optional when it comes to cremation. If there is no interment in a cemetery there is no need to transport flowers, family, minister and casket to the cemetery. However, if one chooses to embalm the body and hold a viewing, one will have to pay for a viewing, embalming and either the rental or purchase of a casket for the viewing.

The cheapest service provided by a funeral home is usually referred to as "immediate cremation, no service." This usually involves the funeral home collecting the body, cremating it and returning the ashes to the family. There is no viewing and no service prior to the cremation, and the funeral home does not organize a service. Many funeral homes advertise very low-priced immediate cremation, no service packages. While the prices are attractive, it is worthwhile to make sure that no costly, but required, additional services or products are involved. Comparison shopping for a cremation can be difficult because some funeral homes separate costs, while others lump them together. A home that offers immediate cremation for $460 sounds better than one that offers it for $890. But if the $890 includes preparation of the body and a cremation container, then it may in fact be a better deal (particularly if the company selling the $460 cremation insists that you use its $695 cremation container).

Most of the services listed in the sidebar are optional. The only fees that are likely to be required relate to transportation, cremation, preparation of the body and the cremation container.

Potential Cremations Costs

Funeral Home Costs
- Embalming: $300 to $600.
- Sanitation. Dressing, casketing and cosmetology: $125 to $165.
- Rental of a viewing casket ($950) and liner ($915).
- Viewing/visitation: $124 to $325. These fees are higher on weekends and in the evening.
- Removal of pacemaker: $75.
- The cremation fee: $600 or higher.
- A cremation container. This can range from $100 to $5000.
- Transportation. Transportation can involve taking the body to funeral home, taking to the body to the crematory, taking the ashes to the location of the service, a limousine for the family and a flower car. At one funeral home, the fee for the hearse, which carried the funeral director and the minister was $165, the limousine for family was $125 and a second limousine was $225.
- Urns: $150 to $33,245.
- Urn personalization: $50 and up.

Cemetery Costs
- Cremation lot in cemetery. A plot for a single urn at a Winnipeg cemetery was $485. At a British Columbia cemetery the cost of an interment lot was $735.
- Perpetual-care fund: depends on cost of the lot.
- Interment in a cemetery lot: $200 and up (fees are higher on weekends).
- Cremation urn vaults: $160 to $1345.
- Columbarium niche. A Winnipeg cemetery charged $1815 for its premium outdoor niches. Another Winnipeg cemetery charged around $3000 for an indoor niche for two.
- Opening and closing a columbarium niche: $250.
- Ossuary: A Regina cemetery charged $207 to scatter at its ossuary.
- Ossuary and memorialization: A Regina Cemetery charged $483 to scatter at the ossuary and have the deceased included on the ossuary memorial.
- Depositing the ashes in a memorial bench in a cemetery: $2000 to $6000.
- Scattering in a cemetery scattering garden: $35 to $125. Some cemeteries also require the purchase of a small marker that is displayed near the scattering ground.

Memorialization
- Marker: $400 to $500, but $1000 is not uncommon for a modest bronze marker.
- Marker base: $300 and up.
- Installation of marker and base: $200.

One might also expect to be charged a fee for the services of the funeral director, staff and overhead. If the funeral home staff is also involved in arranging the funeral service, there might be an additional service fee as well.

CHAPTER 11

A SERVICE TO HONOUR THE DEAD

WHAT IS A SERVICE?

SERVICES ARE OPTIONAL. THERE IS no legal requirement for any sort of service to honour the dead or, to use the increasingly common term, celebrate the life of the deceased. If the deceased leaves no family or close friends, it might well make sense not to have a service. For the religiously observant, a service is usually not optional, since it is one of the most significant forms of religious observation, giving those whom you have left behind one last opportunity to say a prayer for the fate of your soul.

Even if you are not counting on your friends to plead your case with the Almighty, funeral services can perform a range of important functions that benefit the living. A funeral allows people to re-establish their relationships with the deceased, gives survivors a chance to affirm shared values, deal with any guilt they feel for having survived and reflect on the deceased's entire life (as opposed to the final illness). Finally, and perhaps most significantly, it allows people to provide each other with emotional support in a time of need.[1] These are not small matters, and one should think carefully before giving an instruction that there be no service following one's death.

There are three basic types of service:

- a funeral service
- a memorial service
- a committal service.

A funeral service is a service that takes place with the presence of the body of the deceased (either in an open or closed casket), while a memorial service takes place without the body being present. Because the act of cremation constitutes the final disposition of the body, the service that takes place in the presence of cremated remains is a memorial service as opposed to a funeral service. Often the focus of a memorial service is on the life lived rather than on the fate of the body. Such services also provide a greater opportunity for a more spontaneous involvement in the service. A committal service is held either at the graveside or in a crematory chapel.

The word "service" does not imply a religious service: a funeral, memorial or committal service can be secular or religious.

RELIGIOUS SERVICES

For the religiously observant, many of the decisions about the form of service are in large measure not up for discussion — all religions have developed rituals to help people navigate their passage through life's great transitions. Services obviously vary from faith to faith, but it is useful to remember that a religious funeral is at heart a religious service and not a celebration of the life of the person who has died.

The eulogy, in which a friend or family member pays tribute to the deceased, is a relatively new development in North American funerals. And they are meeting with growing opposition from both religious leaders and funeral directors, one of whom compares the growth of eulogies to a karaoke night and some people's inability to resist an open mike. Funeral directors argue that the growth in eulogies, particularly at services where a general invitation is issued for anyone who wishes to share their memories, has added to the length of funerals. For religious leaders, the issue is more complex. A religious funeral service is not intended to leave people questioning why God would give us such a wonderful friend only to snatch him away. The sight of a close friend or spouse breaking down in tears while delivering a eulogy can be moving and even cathartic, but it is at odds with the church's message that the deceased may well be in a better place.[2]

As surprising as it might seem, it is not uncommon in some congregations for the minister or priest to not even mention the name of the deceased, since in death we are all equal. Faiths that do not allow eulogies as a part of the service are often open to the giving a eulogy either immediately before or after a service. While the Roman Catholic Church has dropped much of its opposition to cremation, the preference is still for the body to be present in a casket during the funeral mass.

WHERE TO HOLD A SERVICE

Location is to some measure a function of the type of service being held. Funeral services are usually held in a place of worship or funeral home, partly because those buildings are equipped for moving a casket in and out of their premises, and they have lots of parking. Since a memorial service does not involve a casket, the service can be held in a home, hotel, restaurant, art gallery, pub, park, garden, boat, cemetery, place of worship, funeral home — or even a golf course. Some golf courses have so many services or scattering of ashes that players complain about the disruption of their games. In England, the Manchester City Football Club not only has a special scattering garden for cremations, it actively markets itself as a place where families can hold full funeral services. The website of the funeral home that organizes the funerals asks, "Where better to pay tribute to a loved one's life than a place where they spent many happy hours with family and friends following their team?"[3]

Some funeral homes lower costs by not having their own chapel, instead renting local halls or churches. This allows them to save money on the upkeep of a hall and the cost of owning and maintaining a large parking lot. For their part, many corporate funeral homes, all of which own large chapels, do not give a price break if they are asked to arrange the service in a local hall rather than in their chapel. It is their position that outside funerals cost them more than ones held in their chapel.

INVENTING A FUNERAL SERVICE

Funeral services present a challenge to those who do not belong to any faith. To address the needs of this growing number of people, funeral directors are increasingly serving as event planners, working with the family to establish what sort of event would be appropriate. The lack of a tradition to fall back on can be particularly stressful. Not only must the family deal with the loss, it must develop its own ceremony. As Neil Bardal notes, "The baby boomers are going to transform this business. For years we sold the traditional funeral. But now we are dealing with people who want to do it their way. And they want to do death their way."

A growing number of people market themselves as "funeral celebrants." The Oklahoma City-based In-Sight Institute was established in 1999 by Doug Manning, a former Baptist minister, to train and license funeral celebrants. As the name suggests, a celebrant leads what is meant to be a celebration of the life of the deceased. One such celebrant, Norma Wellwood of Vancouver, organized a service that included giveaways of licorice twists and jujubes to celebrate a grandmother with a passion for treats. At another service, the family of a woman who loved to hike gave attendees stones from an area close to her home.[4]

United Church Minister Karen Toole of Winnipeg said that she was once auditioned by a local man who was choosing someone to preside over his funeral. If you are not affiliated with a congregation, but wish to have a religious ceremony, most funeral homes are able to provide references to ministers from various faiths who will conduct a service for a small fee.

In planning a service you may wish to include traditions that spring from organizations to which you have belonged, such as the military, service organizations or trade unions. A military service, for example, might include flags, buglers and an honour guard. The digital communications revolution of recent times has opened the door to an almost unlimited number of ways to memorialize the dead, from slide shows playing on computer screens to PowerPoint presentations.

RECEPTION

A service is usually followed by a reception. Depending on the size of the turnout and budget, this can be held in the funeral home, church hall, a private home or just about any facility that can be rented. Aside from the hall rental, the major cost is for catering and staffing the facility. This is one area where a funeral director's experience as an event planner may be of real assistance to a family.

The following is a listing of the decisions that have to be addressed in planning a service:

- Do you want a funeral service, a memorial service or a graveside service?
- Do you want a secular service or a religious service?
- Whom would you like to preside over the service?
- Whom would you like to give the eulogy?
- Do you wish to have anything special read at the service?
- Are there pieces of music you would like to have sung or played at the service?
- Are there musicians or singers that you would like to perform at the service?
- Do you want it to be a public service or a private service?
- Where will the service be held?
- Are there any cultural traditions that you wish to see honoured?
- Are there any photos that you wish to have displayed? Will there be an audio-visual? If so, who will prepare it?
- Is there a message that you would like to have read out — or played back either on audio or videotape?
- Who should be the pallbearers?

It is very difficult to give price estimates on most of these items since the costs vary significantly. Costs related to the service can include the following:

- The rental of a chapel or hall ($200 for a church). Alderwoods in Winnipeg charges $690 for coordinating and directing a funeral or memorial service, either in its facility or an offsite facility,
- The fee for the minister: $150 to $500.
- The fee organist and soloist: $100 and up.
- Rental of a reception hall. This cost will vary depending on location and the size of hall.
- Catering. Costs will vary by location.

- Staff. Expect to pay at least a hostess fee.
- A sign-in book. Some people chose to have different books for the visitation and the ceremony.
- Prayer card/program to give to mourners. These can be printed up on a home computer for the cost of the paper or be high-end printing jobs.
- Thank-you cards to send those who attend the ceremony. There are wide ranges of options from doing up cards on a home computer or downloading cards from various websites (and even e-mailed to those who attended the funeral) to having special cards printed. Funeral homes sell cards, but you might get a better price elsewhere.
- Flowers. Again, the price will vary dramatically from place to place.

OBITUARIES AND DEATH NOTICES

In addition to the service and the reception, another cost common to many funerals is the obituary or death notice. Technically, an obituary is a news story about the death of a prominent person. News staff write them and there is no charge to the family. However, the family has no input into what the article says; and, of course, most of us do not rate an obituary.

A death notice is a paid advertisement that is written and paid for by the estate or the family. Along with a biography, it usually includes information about any planned service and charities to which memorial donations can be made.

People are usually surprised at the cost of publishing a newspaper death notice. The *Winnipeg Free Press* charges approximately forty dollars an inch and ninety dollars for a photograph. Given the narrowness of the columns in the death sections of most newspapers, even a relatively short notice will cost upwards of a hundred dollars. As part of a funeral plan, it is helpful to record the sort of background information that family members would find difficult to track down in the short time they usually have to compose a death notice. Having at hand the full names of parents, date of birth, association memberships, places of employment, places of residence and the proper spellings of the names of all the relatives who should be mentioned makes the composition of a death notice less stressful. Preparing information for a death notice also provides an opportunity to identify charities to which survivors can be encouraged to make donations.

When determining the cost of a funeral you should be aware that a funeral director can arrange a number of indirect services. These could include organizing newspaper death notices, paying the clergy, and arranging and paying for flowers. Such costs are usually referred to as cash disbursements.

OVER-PLANNING

It could be a mistake to have too detailed a plan for a funeral or memorial service. These services are part of the tribute that the living pay the dead. While it is important that your wishes be known and respected, your survivors deserve an opportunity to shape your memorial.

CHAPTER 12

PAYING FOR YOUR FUNERAL

THIS CHAPTER LOOKS AT THE QUESTIONS related to financing a funeral. It starts with the simple question of who pays for a funeral and then outlines a number of benefits for which people might apply to defray those costs. This is followed by a discussion of the far more complex question of when to pay for a funeral, examining both the different ways in which you can prepay your funeral and whether there is any financial advantage in so doing.

WHO PAYS FOR A FUNERAL?

Legally, the person who enters into a contract with a funeral home, cemetery, crematory or other service provider is the person who has to pay for the funeral and cemetery goods and services. In the case of pre-bought services, the person enters into a contract prior to death and establishes either a trust fund or an insurance policy to pay for the service, although a number of goods can be purchased outright. If no goods and services have been bought in advance, the usual process is for a family member to enter into a contract with service providers in the expectation of being repaid by the estate. One can be certain that when a person approaches a funeral director to arrange a funeral for someone else, the director will be trying to determine if the family member has the legal authority to arrange the funeral and the financial ability to pay for the funeral that is being arranged.

WHAT BENEFITS ARE AVAILABLE TO HELP PAY FOR A FUNERAL?

A number of benefits exist to assist in paying for a funeral. If applicable, these are usually paid out only upon application of the executor of the deceased's estate. These opportunities are as follows:

- The Canada Pension Plan allows a maximum of $2500 death benefit if the deceased paid into the plan. Call 1-800-277-9914 for information.
- Provincial social assistance programs provide a benefit for deceased program recipients.
- The Department of Indian and Northern Affairs provides assistance if the deceased has status under the *Indian Affairs Act* and was receiving income assistance at the time of death.
- The Last Post Fund, under certain circumstances, provides assistance for the funeral of a veteran. Call 1-800-465-7113 for information.

In the case of deaths resulting from workplace injuries or traffic accidents, workers compensation funds and automobile insurers generally provide death benefits. In addition, the deceased's estate may be eligible for fraternal, union or employer benefits.

WHEN SHOULD YOU PAY FOR A FUNERAL?

Few people in the deathcare industry make any distinction between pre-planning and pre-buying a funeral. In the 1960s, cemeteries were the only sector of the deathcare industry that pre-sold their products, employing a small army of door-to-door salespeople. Increasingly, the funeral industry has focussed on pre-need sales as opposed to the delivery of at-need service. A growing number of the people working in the funeral industry are not embalmers or service providers but salespeople who earn a commission when they pre-sell a funeral. In some ways, the selling of the service has come to overshadow the provision of the service in many large funeral corporations. Hewitt Helmsing, who spent much of his life in the funeral industry, running his own funeral home in Regina and working for the Loewen Group and SCI, says that in the corporate funeral homes "the professional embalmer was paid a heck of a lot less than the commissioned salespeople, and this caused a great deal of discontent." Neil Bardal comments that it also means that the people who are pre-selling services do not have an intimate understanding of what they are selling.

THE BENEFITS OF PAY NOW, DIE LATER

The industry presents the following arguments for paying for your funeral and your cemetery lot in advance:

- One can lock in today's price, gaining protection from inflation.
- The deceased's family will not have to make expensive decisions and shop around for a funeral home at a stressful time.
- It allows people to comparison shop and choose the funeral home they want.
- People can control the amount that will be spent on the funeral.

HOW CAN YOU PREPAY?

One can purchase certain funeral-related goods such as a casket, a grave marker and a cemetery lot for cash. Under this sort of arrangement, the purchaser becomes the outright owner and often takes delivery of the product, although cemeteries are often prepared to store products such as markers. One can also enter into time-payment arrangements for a number of cemetery products. For example, lots and niches in City of Winnipeg cemeteries can be purchased over a one-year period, provided there is a 25 percent deposit. The city does not allow the lot or niche to be used until it is paid for in full.

There are a number of funeral products — embalming and cremation being particularly good examples — of which most people would prefer not to take advance delivery. Trust funds and insurance policies are essentially tools intended to allow you to create savings that will be used to purchase these goods and services.

The trust fund or insurance policy approaches generally involve entering into a pre-arranged funeral contract with a funeral home or taking out an insurance policy and a funeral contract with a funeral home. The contract or the policy may or may not provide price guarantees. The trust fund is a tool that allows one to save money to pay for the funeral. In essence, it does not pay out more than one puts into it. Insurance policies, on the other hand, should pay out the full amount for which it was purchased. In some cases, this guarantee might not come into effect until you have paid premiums for a specified period of time.

Guaranteed Items

For those items specified as guaranteed there should be no extra charges at the time of death (providing all the terms of payment have been met). The funeral director will calculate the cost of the specified services at the then-current value. If the cost is greater than the amount in the trust or specified in the insurance policy, the funeral home cannot charge the difference for the guaranteed goods and services. In some jurisdictions, if the cost is less than the amount in the trust or specified in the insurance policy, the estate receives a refund. It can happen that certain goods or services that were specified when the contract was taken out are not available at the time of death. If the contract is guaranteed, the funeral home is required to supply goods and services that are at least equal in value to the services that had been contracted for, or provide a partial refund.

Non-guaranteed Items

In the case of a non-guaranteed contract, the funeral home is allowed to charge the difference between the amount of money in the trust account or the value of the insurance policy and the cost of the services provided. The services that this policy applies to are usually services that are not within the direct control of the funeral director.[1]

In arranging either a trust fund or an insurance policy, it is useful to determine which costs are included and which prices are being guaranteed.

Financing Through a Trust Fund

In a trust fund arrangement the funeral home places money paid to it into a trust fund on the understanding that the money is to be used to pay for funeral goods and services in the future. At the time of arranging the trust, the purchaser and funeral home agree on a pre-arranged funeral contract that lists the items to be supplied and their cost. These contracts usually do not involve the cemetery lot or marker. One can make one lump-sum payment or a series of regular payments into a trust fund (usually the full amount is to be paid within five years) to pay for the items listed in this contract.

These trust funds are regulated by provincial governments and covered by the Canada Deposit Insurance Corporation. One can back out of one these agreements and receive a full refund within a set period (often within thirty days of entering into the agreement). Beyond that point, the funeral home is required to place the money into a trust and provide the purchaser with an investment receipt. If the purchaser dies before the full amount has been paid into the trust, the amount that is in the trust is paid towards the funeral and the estate is required to make up the difference. If the purchaser dies after the full amount is paid into the trust, the funeral home is required to deliver the agreed-upon service. The investment (and any interest it may have earned) is distributed according to provincial regulation. In Ontario any excess over the current price of the services is returned to the family; in some other provinces the funeral home is allowed to retain the surplus.

One can usually still cancel a trust contract after the initial thirty-day cooling-off period; however, one is likely to receive only a partial refund. In Prince Edward Island, for example, after the thirty-day grace period, purchasers are entitled to 88 percent of the deposit if they cancel during the first three years. After three years, they are entitled to 100 percent of the money deposited plus the interest.[2] In Ontario the funeral home can, on cancellation, retain 10 percent of the money, up to $200. The financial institution can also charge a cancellation fee.

It is possible to transfer a pre-arranged funeral contract and the associated trust fund from one funeral home to another home, but one usually needs the agreement of the funeral director to whom the agreement is being transferred.[3]

Arbor Memorial Services reports that, on average, there is an eight-year gap between the time a person enters into a trust arrangement and the date on which the company has to deliver the service. In 2004 it had set aside (in the case of pre-bought items) or placed into trust $158.8 million in pre-bought cemetery services and $179.2 million in pre-bought funeral services.[4]

Financing Through an Insurance Company

There are two types of funeral insurance policies: pre-need insurance (actually a group annuity policy administered by an insurance company) and whole-life insurance. The first is available through funeral homes while insurance agents sell the latter. With pre-need insurance, the purchaser agrees to make monthly payments for a specified period; at the end of that period they no longer have to make payments but remain insured. With whole life, the payments are lower but coverage ceases as soon as one stops making payments. Health-related issues also affect insurance policy rates and eligibility. Rates can be higher for people with health problems and companies may decline to insure if there is a health problem or decline to pay out if they conclude that there was a misrepresentation of a health problem.

Pre-need insurance

Pre-need insurance policies are usually payable to the funeral director upon proof of death. In other words, the funeral home is the beneficiary of the policy on the purchaser's life. Pre-need insurance purchasers usually have up to ten years to make all their payments, while people who finance their funeral through a trust fund are expected to make all their payments within five years. This means that, for the same funeral, pre-need insurance payments are usually lower than trust-fund payments. However, the total amount that the purchaser pays for the policy over ten years is likely to be more than a person would be required to pay into a trust to provide for the same funeral goods and services.

Insurance premium payments are not placed in trust and are not refundable, although one can usually cancel the contract and get a refund within the first thirty days.[5] If one were to decide to cancel the policy after five years, there would be no refund, but one would have been insured during those five years.

Prepaying a funeral by pre-need insurance policy can involve two contracts. A contract with the insurance company outlines the amount of the life insurance policy (usually the contracts refer to product being purchased as an annuity). A second contract with the funeral home outlines the funeral services and supplies that it is required to provide for the value of the insurance policy. It will state which prices are guaranteed. It should be noted that failure to make a payment can void those guarantees.

While funeral homes will assist in arranging the purchase of pre-need insurance, they are not directly selling insurance. Large corporations such as Assurant Solutions sell the insurance policies. From 1998 to 2000 Assurant (or as it was then known, American Memorial Life) was owned by the funeral conglomerate Service Corporation International.[6] While the funeral homes do not sell the policies, they do receive administrative and marketing allowances from the insurance companies. In 2004 Arbor Memorial Services had $79.1 million in pre-need funeral contracts receivable from insurance companies.[7]

Whole life insurance

Whole-life insurance policies to pay for funerals are relatively new in Canada. In 2003, General Electric's Insource Limited, EDS and Western Life Insurance

Company of Canada launched Everest, which it described as "first nation-wide funeral package."[8] Everest offers three whole-life insurance policies, valued at $5000, $7500 and $10,000. If one meets the health qualifications, the payments are based on age and sex. For example, a $5000 policy would cost a fifty-two-year-old male thirty-three dollars a month or a single payment of $4497. After ten years the monthly payments would amount to $3960. However, the purchaser would have to keep on making monthly payments to keep the policy valid. If the fifty-two-year-old lived to the age of eighty-two, he would have paid $11,880 to get $5000 worth of insurance. (For a fifty-two-year-old woman, the prices would be thirty dollars a month or a $4194 single payment. The ten-year cost would be $3600 and the thirty-year cost would be $10,800 for $5000 worth of insurance.)

It is possible to receive a partial refund from policies of this sort, but because no advance agreement is entered into with a funeral home, there are no price guarantees — the purchaser is not locking in today's prices.[9] Whole-life insurance offers the lowest payments when compared to trusts or pre-need insurance. However, there is no cap on the length of time that the purchaser must make payments to maintain coverage, nor is there a guarantee of what the insurance will buy.

WHAT ARE THE DISADVANTAGES OF PRE-BUYING YOUR FUNERAL?

Pre-buying What You May Not Need
Purchasing in advance does lock in today's price (under certain circumstances), but it also requires you to spend today's money for goods that you may not enjoy (if that is the appropriate word) for many years.

Pre-buying Makes It Harder to Change Your Funeral Plan
While you should make a funeral plan, you should also be able to change the plan easily and quickly. An average married couple pre-buying thirty years ago would likely have paid for a double lot, embalming and two caskets. But today, when the couple is likely to be making use of any pre-bought services, it is more likely they want a cremation, no embalming and only a single lot in which to bury the ashes (if they do not wish to have them scattered). It will be difficult and costly for the couple to get out of these prepaid arrangements without losing money. People who have pre-bought the cemetery lot, the casket and the headstone might find it difficult to find a buyer. These are personalized items that are likely to be sold at a loss. Additionally, some cemeteries have fairly strict bylaws that limit the ability to resell lots.

If You Buy Too Far in Advance, You May Lose Track of the Purchase
Jane Saxby, Winnipeg's cemetery administrator, noted that families do not necessarily make use of all the lots that they purchase. For this reason, she said it is worthwhile to contact any cemeteries at which family members

have been buried to determine whether your family has burial rights there. Otherwise people end up paying twice for burial rights.

The Funeral Home May Change Ownership and Philosophy
The funeral home or cemetery may go out of business or be sold. You might arrange your funeral with your kindly community funeral home, but when your children come to put your plan into effect, they could well be dealing with new corporate owners who are more interested in upselling them than honouring your initial plan. The funeral home can do this because while it is required to provide at least what you contracted for (in the case of a guaranteed contract), your estate is not bound by your instructions. Your distraught family members can still buy a more expensive casket or decide to have you embalmed and entombed, even if all you contracted for was immediate cremation, no service.

When You Prepay, You Are Paying Now for a Product That You Will Never See
One hopes a very lengthy time will pass between the day on which you make your final payment and the date on which your estate accepts delivery. Since you will not be around, it will be difficult for your estate to determine whether you have received the product that you thought you were purchasing. For this reason alone, if you do pre-buy, you should attempt to have the person who is named as the executor of your will present when you sign the contract. This will allow her or him an opportunity to find out just what it is that you believe you are buying.

You Will Not Have Access to Money That You Could Otherwise Spend on Yourself and Your Family While You Are Alive
Unless you are planning on an extraordinarily expensive funeral, the odds are that your estate will be sufficient to cover your funeral costs. A 2003 Statistics Canada report states that in 1999 the average net worth of senior families (couples over sixty-five) in Canada was $155,000. Furthermore, only 27 percent of Canadian seniors had debt (and 82 percent of them were comfortable with their level of debt). Older single women had the lowest median net worth: $77,000, compared with $216,000 for senior couples. Finally, only 8 percent of senior families felt that they would not be able to pay for an unexpected expense of $5000. In other words, for most Canadians, there is likely to be enough money in the estate to pay for any reasonably priced funeral.[10]

The Money May Not Be There
When a funeral home in Port au Basque, Newfoundland, went out of business in November 2000, the eighty-eight people who had purchased nearly a half-million dollars worth of pre-paid funerals were left in the lurch. While recent Newfoundland legislation required the establishment of an

industry-subsidized fund to address such situations, the fund had not been created when the home failed. The owner was later convicted of theft and false pretenses, and the provincial funeral industry stepped in to honour the outstanding contracts. An investigation by the Newfoundland provincial auditor showed that two years after the passage of the *Prepaid Funeral Services Act*, which required the licensing of all Newfoundland funeral homes, only twenty-eight of ninety-one provincial homes had applied for licences. While twenty-seven had been licensed, the auditor concluded that only four were in full compliance with the Act.[11]

The Commissioned Sales System Is Open for Abuse
The following two examples, both from Winnipeg, demonstrate how the commission sales system is open to abuse and misinformation. A woman with a number of severe and obvious health problems was contacted by a corporate funeral home representative shortly after her mother was buried at one of the funeral home's Winnipeg cemeteries. While she initially indicated that she was not interested in pre-arranging a funeral, the salesperson was persistent. The woman eventually arranged a funeral that was to be paid for through an insurance policy that she also purchased with the assistance of the salesperson. Unfortunately for her family, from whom I heard the story, the policy clearly stated that a person with her health conditions was ineligible for the insurance policy that she had purchased — at the time of purchase she was bedridden, largely unable to read due to eye infections. When she died, the company refused to honour the policy, even though it had collected the payments. The insurance company's position was that she had provided inaccurate information on her insurance application; the family's position was that the funeral home representative had assisted her in filling out the form and would have been aware of the inaccuracies and her ineligibility. Neither the funeral home nor the insurance company was prepared to accept responsibility for having sold her an inappropriate policy (although the insurance company did note that it sells a more expensive policy that would have been more appropriate to her needs).

In the summer of 2006 an Alderwoods funeral home invited me out to their location to provide me with a copy of their free estate planner. It took their "family service professional" about ten minutes to go through the estate planning kit, which stresses the importance of having a will and compiling lists of your insurance polices, bank accounts and investments, outlines various benefits that could be available upon death and concludes with a list of the sort of information that a family member would need to write an obituary and register a death. It also contains a list of sixty-seven things that must be done when someone dies. (These types of lists are overwhelming — Arbor Memorial Services list eighty-seven, and I have seen others that put it at one hundred.) At that point, the family service professional morphed into a salesperson. She launched into a carefully scripted presentation on the value of pre-planning your funeral, which took as its starting point the fact that we try to plan for all the big and expensive events in our life. In this presentation, pre-planning and prepaying were seen as identical.

She told me at Alderwoods, a traditional service would cost $3460, plus $3000 for a casket, $2000 for incidentals (the reception, food, obituaries, clergy, etc.) for a total of $8460. On top of that would be the cost of a cemetery lot ($1300 at any of the three cemeteries that Alderwoods operate in Winnipeg), $3000 for a marker and $1500 for a vault (all their cemeteries require liners or vaults). She said that I could get by with an $800 grave liner, but for her money, a vault was a sound investment. Cremation (including a required $700 cremation casket, a modest $305 urn and all of the incidentals) would run me $6895. With cremation there was no need to buy a plot or use a columbarium; one's ashes could be scattered in the cemetery's scattering garden for $235.

In the end, she said that the total cost of a funeral was likely to run about $10,000 (that is, without cemetery costs). After asking how old I was and when my father died, she said, "Given the fact that the cost of everything doubles every ten years, let's look at the advantage of buying now." She drew up a little chart showing that if I died in ten years time at sixty-two, a traditional funeral would cost my family $20,000, at seventy-two it would be $40,000 and at eighty-two (three years older than my father was at his death) it would cost $80,000. Should medical science keep me going to ninety-two, funeral costs would set my family back $160,000. If I prepaid now, I would be able to pass on a $150,000 savings to my family.

But prices have not been doubling every ten years. According to Statistics Canada, a basket of goods and services that cost $10,000 in 1966 would cost $63,092 in 2006. If, as the Alderwoods representative suggested, prices doubled every ten years, that basket should cost $160,000 in 2006. During the 1989 to 1996 period, the number of deaths in Canada increased by 11 percent, while spending on funerals increased by 18 percent.[12] The moral of the story being that corporate funeral home family service representatives are not giving you financial advice, they are giving you a sales pitch.

Pre-buying Can Create a False Sense of Security
It is important to recognize that it is almost impossible to buy a plan that guarantees and prepays all funeral expenses. Any time I have spoken to people whose parents had pre-bought their funerals, they discovered that when the time came for the funeral, there were additional expenses. This can arise from a number of sources. As noted above, not all costs are guaranteed and not all costs are included in pre-purchase packages. According to Walter Johanson, the executive director of the Memorial Society of British Columbia, "One member on our board said he does not know of anyone whose prepayment plan covered everything."

Saving for it yourself may be more effective

Given these drawbacks it might make just as much economic sense to put aside enough money to pay for a funeral in a guaranteed investment certificate or a Canada Savings Bond. If the investment grows at least as fast as the rate of inflation, you should have enough to pay for a funeral at future prices. According to Norm Larsen, "The best way to control the cost of your funeral is to make a funeral plan, set a price limit and make sure that your next of kin (and any other people who are likely to be involved in carrying out your plan) agree to follow your plan."

If You Do Pre-buy

- Ask to see the seller's licence. Make a note of the name and date on the licence.
- Make sure there is a clear definition of what is covered by the contract. This includes determining which prices are guaranteed and which are not guaranteed.
- Find out if the plan be cancelled at any time? If so, how? Will there be a refund? If so, how is the refund calculated?
- Can you cash in your insurance policy in advance?
- Ask if the plan can be transferred to another province or country.
- Find out what happens if the funeral home goes out of business or is sold.
- What will happen to your money? If there is a trust, how much will be placed in trust?
- Which company will hold the trust and how often will it present you with reports?
- What happens to the money that the trust earns?
- Are your survivors required to use the funeral home named in the prepayment documents or can you or your survivors switch to a different funeral home?
- If switching is allowed what are the costs of doing so?
- Can you change the plan? If so, how?
- What happens if you fail to make a payment on time? Is there an extra charge on late fees?
- What will your estate have to do to claim payment?
- If you have bought a funeral lot will you be allowed to resell it if you choose? Will the cemetery buy it back?

CHAPTER 13

PREPARING A FUNERAL PLAN

THE FOLLOWING FUNERAL PLAN, WITH slight modification, was developed by Norm Larsen.

HOW TO PLAN YOUR FUNERAL

PREPARE AND DISCUSS YOUR PLAN!

1. **Prepare** a written funeral plan. After you fill in the form "My Funeral Plan" (which accompanies this document) you can use it as your plan or you can type or write out just the parts you have filled in on separate pages. If you use "My Funeral Plan" as your plan, do NOT remove any of the numbered pages — that could raise questions about what is missing.

2. **Discuss** your funeral plan with *the people most likely to be involved in arranging your funeral.* Your plan can be carried out **only if those people know about it!** President Franklin Roosevelt's instructions for a simple funeral were found in his desk three days *after* his elaborate state funeral in 1945.

3. **Obtain agreement.** A person who arranges a funeral **usually has no legal duty to follow any instructions left by the deceased**. It is therefore important that *the people who are most likely to arrange your funeral* agree to carry out your plan. In 2003 the famous baseball player Ted Williams died, without leaving a funeral plan; his adult son and daughter squabbled in public on what to do with his body. If you think some people might disagree with your plan, make it clear that you expect your plan to be followed. If agreement is not impossible, consider making your funeral plan part of your will.

4. When your plan is complete, **make copies** of it and give one to some or all of *the people who are most likely to arrange your funeral.*

VISIT **AT LEAST** ONE FUNERAL HOME

5. **Take your plan to at least one funeral home** for suggestions and price quotations that are *itemized and with the cost noted for each item.* It must be itemized to be useful — and to be able to compare it to other quotations. When you go to a funeral home, **go with another person** — perhaps someone who is likely to be involved in arranging your funeral or a friend who also is making a funeral plan or who already has a plan.

CHOOSE A CEMETERY — AND MARKER

6. **If you choose earth burial of your body or ashes, consult cemeteries**. Call the cemetery of your choice. If you don't have a particular cemetery in mind, call a couple of cemetery offices and make an appointment to discuss that part of your plan. See "**Cemeteries**" in the Yellow Pages.

7. **If you want your grave marked** with either a flat marker or upright tombstone, go to two or three places that sell them to obtain brochures, prices and suggestions. See "**Memorials**" in the Yellow Pages.

CHANGES IN YOUR PLAN

8. **Changes**. If you change your plan, tell the people who have copies of it. Consider completing a fresh copy and giving a copy to *the people most likely to arrange your funeral*. If you have a will, make sure that any mention of your funeral is consistent with your funeral plan.

MY FUNERAL PLAN

*Note: you can use this document as your funeral plan, or — **even better** — you can complete it and then write or type out just your choices in a separate (and much shorter) document.*

Full name: _____

Maiden or other name: _____

Address: _____Postal Code _____

Telephone number: _____

PART 1: DONATION FOR MEDICAL EDUCATION OR TRANSPLANT

If you choose the first option, your body will not be used for either medical education or transplant. If any of your organs are accepted for transplant your body will not be accepted for donation for medical education or research. However, you can select either option 2 or 3 and 4. That way, if you are not an organ donor, your body can still be used for medical education or research. If you select either 2 and 4 or 3 and 4, you should make it clear to your family that your preference is to be an organ donor if possible and if not possible to donate your body for research.

No transplant
1. [ ] I do NOT want to donate my body — or any part of it — for medical education or transplant.

Transplant
2. [ ] I want to donate *any part of my body* that can be used for transplant.
3. [ ] I want to donate *the following parts* of my body for transplant (*check off*):
   a) Organs: [ ] heart [ ] kidneys [ ] lungs [ ] bowel [ ] pancreas
      [ ] liver
   b) Tissue: [ ] corneas [ ] skin [ ] heart valves [ ] solid bones and joints

Medical education and research
4. [ ] I want to donate *my entire body* for medical education or scientific research.

PART 2: CREMATION OR EARTH BURIAL

*Note: Even if you want to donate your entire body for medical education, **you must have a backup plan** — in case your body is not accepted. This is the first choice you must make:*

I want my body disposed of by [ ] cremation [ ] earth burial

Note: If you chose cremation, go on to Part 3 (Cremation). If you chose earth burial, go on to Part 4 (Earth Burial).

PART 3: CREMATION

*Note: Complete this section **only if** you have chosen to be cremated.*

A: Type of Service
I want the following type of memorial service or funeral service (*choose ONE*):

    [ ] no service of any kind
    [ ] immediate cremation, followed by a graveside service
    [ ] immediate cremation, followed by a memorial service
    [ ] a funeral service with my body present, followed by cremation

B: Disposal of My Ashes
I want my ashes (*choose ONE*)

    [ ] kept at home until _____ and then _____
    [ ] buried in an urn at _____
    [ ] put in an urn and then placed in a niche in a columbarium at

_____

    [ ] deposited in the ash crypt at _____
    [ ] scattered at (name the place)_____
    [ ] other: _____

C: My Grave
*Note: Complete this **only if** you have chosen to have your ashes buried.*
On my grave, I want (*choose ONE*)

    [ ] no marker or tombstone
    [ ] a flat marker
    [ ] an upright tombstone
    [ ] other: _____

If you have chosen a marker or tombstone, indicate what you want
    inscribed on it: _____

PART 4: EARTH BURIAL
*Note: Complete this section **only** if you have chosen to be buried in a casket.*

I do [ ] do not [ ] want a particular type of casket. _____

A: Type of Service
I want the following type of funeral service:
  [ ] no service of any kind
  [ ] immediate earth burial with a graveside service
  [ ] immediate earth burial, followed by a memorial service
  [ ] a "traditional" funeral service with my body present, followed by earth burial

B: Burial
I want my body buried at (*name of cemetery*): _____

I want these possessions buried with me (*such as a ring, picture or book*):
_____

I want my casket (*choose ONE*)
  [ ] *not* to be placed in a liner or vault
  [ ] to be placed in a cement liner
  [ ] to be placed in a sealed vault, made of _____

C: My Grave
On my grave, I want (*choose ONE*)
  [ ] no marker or tombstone
  [ ] a flat marker
  [ ] an upright tombstone
  [ ] other: _____
If you have chosen a marker or tombstone, indicate what you want
  inscribed on it: _____

PART 5: A SERVICE
*Note: Complete this section **only** if you have chosen to have a service.*

I want the service to be
  [ ] private, attended only by my immediate family
  [ ] open to anyone who wishes to attend
  [ ] other: _____

I want the service to be held (*choose ONE, and give the name or location of the place*)
[ ] in a place of worship [ ] at a funeral home [ ] other (such as at a home, hotel or grave site).

I want the service to be conducted by (*name a person or position*):

_____

I want the service to include the following (*give details on a separate page*):
[ ] flowers [ ] music [ ] readings [ ] prayers [ ] eulogy [ ] other

I prefer that (*choose one — or both*) [ ] flowers be accepted [ ] mourners be invited to make donations to the following organization(s):

_____

PART 6: A FUNERAL SERVICE — WITH MY BODY PRESENT
*Note: Complete this section **only** if you have chosen to have a service with your body present.*

I want my body to be placed in [ ] an open casket [ ] a closed casket

I want my body (*choose ONE*)
    [ ] to be embalmed
    [ ] to be cosmetically restored
    [ ] *not* to be embalmed or cosmetically restored
    [ ] *not* to be exposed to any public or private viewing

I prefer my hair and cosmetics to be done
    [ ] by the funeral home
    [ ] by these people: hair: _____ cosmetics: _____

I want my body dressed
    [ ] in my own clothing (specify):_____
    [ ] in specially purchased clothing: _____
    [ ] in a shroud over clothing: _____
    [ ] in a shroud
    [ ] other: _____

I do [ ] do not [ ] wish to have pallbearers. (*If you do, give details on a separate page.*)

***

I am signing this to confirm that this document contains my instructions on how I want my body to be disposed of. I direct my next of kin and any other person involved in disposing of my body to honour my wishes.

Date: _____Signature: _____

IMPORTANT INFORMATION ABOUT YOU

Note: The following information is for the Registration of Death, a form required by law.

Marital status:
[ ] never married [ ] married [ ] widowed [ ] divorced [ ] separated

If married/widowed/divorced/separated, give the full name of husband or the maiden name of wife: _____

Date and place of marriage: _____

Names of children: _____

Occupation/type of business: _____

Social Insurance Number: _____

Employer: _____

Date and place of birth: _____

Resident in community since: _____ Citizenship: _____

Father's full name and place of birth: _____

Mother's maiden name and place of birth: _____

Branch of military service: _____

Location of military service: _____

Serial number: _____

CHECKLIST OF MORE THINGS TO DO

Check off the ones you have done — and then do the rest!

[ ] I have a **will**.

[ ] I have a **living will** (also known as a *health care directive*). A copy of the form and instructions is available by calling the *Manitoba Seniors and Healthy Aging Secretariat* at 204-945-6565.

[ ] I have started to prepare my own **obituary**.

[ ] I have prepared a **list of items** that I want to be given to certain people or organizations after my death. (If you have a list, consider adding it to your will to make it legally binding.)

[ ] I have prepared a **list of the names** and addresses of relatives, friends and others (including businesses) to be notified of my death.

[ ] I have discussed my **funeral plan** with the people who are most likely to arrange my funeral.

[ ] Those people have a **copy of my funeral plan** or they know where I keep my plan.

The **costs** relating to my funeral can be paid from the following: [ ] my estate [ ] a prepaid plan [ ] insurance [ ] bank account [ ] Canada Pension Plan [ ] other: _____

Information about the above matters and about bank accounts, safety deposit box (and key), real estate, credit cards, income tax records, insurance policies, passport, etc. is located in these places:

_____

WHAT TO DO AFTER YOU HAVE A PLAN

1. Consider **typing or writing out** your funeral plan instead of relying on this form. If you decide to use this form, do NOT remove any pages from it. **A missing page can cause confusion**.

2. **Discuss** your plan with *the people most likely to be involved in arranging our funeral*. Your plan can be carried out only if those people know about it! Try to obtain their agreement.

3. **Go to at least one funeral home** with your plan (take a friend or two) and ask for suggestions and price quotations.

4. If you wish to bury your body or ashes, consult at least one cemetery and one memorial firm. See "**Cemeteries**" and "**Memorials**" in the Yellow Pages.

5. Give a copy of your plan to each of the people who are most likely to arrange your funeral — or tell them where you keep your plan.

6. If you change your plan, give a copy of the new plan to *the people most likely to arrange your funeral* or at least tell them of the changes and where you are keeping your plan.

COLLECT YOUR INFORMATION

If you have had to deal with the estate of a deceased person, you know how difficult it is to find documents — and to figure out what a bunch of keys are for! You can save your family that kind of trouble by buying a binder, dividers and some loose-leaf paper. Under each tab in the binder, you can give detailed information *or* a brief note about where the information is located.

Topics
1. List the contents of your wallet or purse, and the keys on your key chain, and what each is for.
2. Bank accounts, including any safety deposit box (and where the key is).
3. Investments, including bonds and GICs.
4. Pension funds.
5. Life insurance.
6. Tax records.
7. Power of Attorney
8. Health Care Directive (Living Will)
9. Funeral plan
10. Obituary
11. Will
12. Estate. List your assets and debts
13. Miscellaneous. List other documents and their location, such as your passport, birth certificate, house title and house insurance.

APPENDIX

FUNERAL REGULATORS

ALBERTA
Funeral Services Regulatory Board
11810 Kingsway Avenue, Edmonton, AB T5G 0X5
Tel.: (403) 452-6130 Toll free: 1-800-563-4652
Fax: (403) 452-6085
Website: www.afsrb.ab.ca

BRITISH COLUMBIA
Business Practices and Consumer Protection Authority
5th Floor, 1019 Wharf Street
P.O. Box 9244. Victoria, BC V8W 9J2
Tel.: (604) 320-1667 Toll free: 1-888-564-9963
Fax: (250) 920-7181
E-mail: info@bpcpa.ca
Website: www.bpcpa.ca

MANITOBA
Board of Administration Under *The Embalmers and Funeral Directors Act*
254 Portage Avenue, Winnipeg, MB R3C 0B6
Tel.: (204) 947-1098 Fax: (204) 945-0424
E-mail: embalmersdirectors@gov.mb.ca

NEW BRUNSWICK
Board for Registration of Embalmers and Funeral Directors
1063 Main Street, P.O. Box 31, Hampton, NB E0G 1Z0
Tel.: (506) 832-5541 Fax: (506) 832-3082

NEWFOUNDLAND AND LABRADOR
Department of Government Services
Consumer and Commercial Affairs Branch
Financial Services Regulation Division
P.O. Box 8700, St. John's, NL A1B 4J6
Tel.: (709) 729-2594 Fax: (709) 729-3205
Website: www.gs.gov.nl.ca/cca/fsr

NOVA SCOTIA
Board of Embalmers and Funeral Directors
P.O. Box 2723, Halifax, NS B3J 3P7
Tel.: (902) 453-5545 Fax: (802) 424-0702
E-mail: nsboard@ns.sympatico.ca

NUNAVUT
Consumer Affairs
Community and Government Services
P.O. Box 440, Baker Lake, NT X0C 0A0
Tel.: (867) 793-3303 Toll free: 1-866-223-8139 Fax: (867) 793-3321
Website: www.gov.nu.ca/Nunavut/English/departments/CGT/

ONTARIO
Board of Funeral Services
Suite 2810, 777 Bay Street, Toronto, ON M5G 2C8
Tel.: (416) 979-5450 Toll free: 1-800-387-4458 Fax: (416) 979-0384
Website: www.funeralboard.com

Cemeteries Regulation Unit
32nd Floor, 250 Yonge Street, Toronto, ON M5B 2N5
Tel.: (416) 326-8800 Toll free: 1-800-889-9768 Fax: (416) 326-8406

PRINCE EDWARD ISLAND
Linda Peters, Compliance Officer
Pre-Arranged Funeral Services Act
Office of the Attorney General
P.O. Box 2000, Charlottetown, PE C1A 7N8
Tel.: (902) 368-5653 Fax: (902) 368-5283
E-mail: lmpeters@gov.pe.ca

QUEBEC
Régie régionale de la santé et des services sociaux
Direction des services techniques et financiers
525 Wilfrid-Hamel Boulevard East
Quebec, QC G1M 2S8
Tel.: (418) 525-1482 Fax: (418) 525-1472
Website: www.msss.gouv.qc.ca

SASKATCHEWAN
Funeral and Cremation Services of Saskatchewan
3847C Albert Street, Regina, SK S4S 3R4
Tel.: (306) 584-1575 Fax: (306) 584-1576
E-mail: sask.funeral@sasktel.net
Website: www.fcscs.ca

YUKON
Department of Community Services
Consumer and Safety Services
P.O. Box 2703, Whitehorse, YT Y1A 2C6
Tel.: (867) 667-5811 Toll free: 1-800-661-0408 (Yukon only) Fax: (867) 393-6295
E-mail: consumer@gov.yk.ca
Website: www.community.gov.yk.ca

TRANSPLANT PROGRAMS IN CANADA

Northern Alberta/Northwest Territories / Nunavut
Human Organ Procurement and Exchange Program (HOPE)
Tel.: (780) 407-1970

Southern Alberta
Human Organ Procurement and Exchange Program (HOPE)
Tel.: (403) 944-8700

British Columbia
British Columbia Transplant Society
Tel.: (604) 877-2240 Toll free: 1-800-663-6189
Website: www.transplant.bc.ca

Manitoba
Manitoba Transplant Program
Tel.: (204) 787-7379

Ontario
Organ Donation Ontario
Tel.: (416) 351-7328 Toll free: 1-800-263-2833

Quebec
Transplant Québec
Toll free: 1-877-463-6366
Website: www.quebec-transplant.qc.ca

Saskatchewan
Saskatchewan Transplant Program
Tel.: (306) 655-5054

New Brunswick
Organ/Tissue Procurement Program
Tel.: (506) 643-6848

Newfoundland and Labrador
Health Sciences Centre, St. John's
Tel.: (707) 777-6600

Nova Scotia / Prince Edward Island
Multi-Organ Transplant Program
Tel.: (902) 473-6193
http://www.cdha.nshealth.ca/transplantservices

Yukon
Yukon Transplant Program
Tel.: (867) 667-3673

NOTES

INTRODUCTION
1. Canada, *Deaths, 2003,* Statistics Canada, Health Statistics Division, 2004, pp. 7–8.
2. Ibid., pp. 14–15.
3. Ibid.

PART ONE: BIG DEATH IN CANADA

CHAPTER 1
1. Elizabeth Lycar and Lorrie Guymer Hutton, *Quite an Undertaking: The Story of Violet Guymer, Canada's First Female Licensed Funeral Director*, Nip & Tuck, 1996, p. 46.
2. James J. Farrell, *Inventing the American Way of Death, 1830–1920*, Temple University Press, 1980, p. 147.
3. Laura Goodman Salverson, *Confessions of an Immigrant's Daughter*, University of Toronto Press, 1981, pp. 98–100.
4. Gary Laderman, *Rest in Peace: A Cultural History of Death and the Funeral Home in Twentieth-century America*, Oxford University Press, 2003, p. 78.
5. Laderman, *Rest in Peace*, p. 14.
6. John L. Konofes and Michael K. McGee, "Old Cemeteries, Arsenic, and Health Safety," *Cultural Resources Management* 19, 10 (1996), pp. 15–18.
7. Lycar and Hutton, *Quite an Undertaking*, p. 125.
8. Farrell, *Inventing the American Way of Death*, p. 175.
9. Herbert C. Northcott and Donna M. Wilson, *Dying and Death in Canada*, Garamond Press, 2001, p. 16.
10. Jennifer Brown, *Strangers in Blood: Fur Trade Company Families in Indian Country*, University of British Columbia Press, 1980, p. 68.
11. Renée Fossett, *In Order to Live Untroubled: Inuit of the Central Arctic, 1550 to 1940*, University of Manitoba Press, 2001, p. 230.
12. Northcott and Wilson, *Dying and Death in Canada*, pp. 14–18.
13. Victor P. Lytwyn, *Muskekowuck Athinuwick: Original People of the Great Swampy Land*, University of Manitoba Press, 2002, p. 168.
14. Northcott and Wilson, *Dying and Death in Canada*, p. 21.
15. Peter N. Moogk, "Les Petits Sauvages: The Children of Eighteenth Century New France," in *Childhood and Family in Canadian History,* Joy Parr (ed.), McClelland and Stewart, 1982, p. 20.
16. Judith Fingard, "The Poor in Winter: Seasonality and Society in Pre-Industrial Canada," in *Readings in Canadian Social History, Volume 2: Pre-Industrial Canada*, Michael S. Cross and Gregory S. Kealey (eds.), McClelland and Stewart, 1982, p. 69.
17. Margaret Conrad, "Recording Angels: The Private Chronicles of Women from the Maritime Provinces of Canada, 1750–1950," in *Essays in Canadian Women's History, Volume Two, The Neglected Majority*, Allison Prentice and Susan Mann Trofimenkoff (eds.), McClelland and Stewart, 1985, p. 47.

18. Conrad, "Recording Angels," p. 55.
19. Bettina Bradbury, "Fragmented Family: Family strategies in the face of death, illness, and Poverty, Montreal, 1860–1885," in *Childhood and Family in Canadian History*, p. 113.
20. Northcott and Wilson, *Dying and Death in Canada*, p. 26.
21. Farrell, *Inventing the American Way of Death*, 148–149.
22. Ibid., 172.
23. Laderman, *Rest in Peace*, p. 18.
24. Farrell, *Inventing the American Way of Death*, p. 152.
25. Thomas E. Kelly and Evan B. Johnson, *The Evolution of the American Funeral Director*, Traverauld Press, 1938, p. 3, cited in Laderman, *Rest in Peace*, p. 11.
26. *Funeral Customs Through the Ages*, F.C. Riddle and Brothers Casket Company, 1929, cited in Laderman, *Rest in Peace*, p. 23.
27. *Embalmer's Monthly*, May 1892, cited in Farrell, *Inventing the American Way of Death*, p. 179.
28. Farrell, *Inventing the American Way of Death*, p. 157.
29. Ibid., p. 181.
30. Immanuel Wallerstein, *Historical Capitalism*, Verso, 1983.
31. Mark Twain, *Life on the Mississippi*, Harper, 1917, p. 348.
32. John Gebhart, *Funeral Costs, What They Average; Are They Too High; Can They Be Reduced?* Putnam, 1928, p. 221, cited in Laderman, *Rest in Peace*, p. 56.
33. Laderman, *Rest in Peace*, pp. 57–58.

CHAPTER 2

1. Jessica Mitford, "St. Peter, Don't You Call Me," in *Poison Penmanship: The Gentle Art of Muckraking*, Random House, 1979, p. 50.
2. Jessica Mitford, *The American Way of Death*, Simon and Schuster, 1963, p. viii.
3. Ibid., p. 13.
4. Ibid., p. 17.
5. "The Furor Over Funerals: Why the Cry of Scandal?" cited in Laderman, *Rest in Peace*, p. xxviii.
6. Laderman, *Rest in Peace*, pp. 114–118.
7. Laderman, *Rest in Peace*, p. xxiv.
8. Stephen R. Prothero, *Purified by Fire: A History of Cremation in America*, University of California Press, 2001, pp. 5–6.
9. Prothero, *Purified by Fire*, pp. 10–21.
10. Prothero, *Purified by Fire*, pp. 25–26.
11. Prothero, *Purified by Fire*, p. 74.
12. Prothero, *Purified by Fire*, pp. 110, 125, 149–150.
13. Brian Young, *Respectable Burial: Montreal's Mount Royal Cemetery*, McGill-Queen's University Press, 2003, pp. 130–131.
14. Young, *Respectable Burial*, pp. 125–127.
15. Young, *Respectable Burial*, pp. 130–139.
16. Allen Mills, *Fool for Christ: The Political Thought of J.S. Woodsworth*, University of Toronto Press, 1991, pp. 252–253.
17. Prothero, *Purified by Fire*, p. 153.
18. Phillip Hewett, *Unitarians in Canada*, Fitzhenry and Whiteside, 1978.

19. Memorial Society of British Columbia, http://www.memorialsocietybc.org/c/about.html, accessed on February 3, 2006.
20. Xavier Cronin, *Grave Exodus: Tending to Our Dead in the 21st century*, Barricade Books, 1995, p. 235.
21. Hewett, *Unitarians in Canada*, pp. 238–239.
22. Prothero, *Purified by Fire*, p. 189.
23. Laderman, *Rest in Peace*, p. 202.
24. Prothero, *Purified by Fire*, p. 195.
25. Laderman, *Rest in Peace*, p. 203.
26. For information on The Simple Alternative, see http://www.thesimplealternative.ca/about_us/about_tsa_history.asp, accessed on March 23, 2007.

CHAPTER 3
1. Philippe Aries, *Western Attitudes Toward Death: From the Middle Ages to the Present*, trans. by Patricia M. Ranum, Johns Hopkins University Press, 1974, p. 22.
2. Friedrich Engels, *The Condition of the Working Class in England*, Panther, 1969, pp. 315–316.
3. Young, *Respectable Burial*, p. 10.
4. Ibid., pp. 9–10.
5. Ibid., pp. 15–16.
6. James J. Farrell, *Inventing the American Way of Death, 1830–1920*, Temple University Press, 1980, p. 105.
7. Cited in Young, *Respectable Burial*, p. 16.
8. Young, *Respectable Burial*, pp. 23–25.
9. Ibid., p. 47.
10. Ibid., p. 34.
11. Ibid., p. 112.
12. Ibid., pp. 116–117.
13. Ibid., p. 121.
14. Tad Friend, "The Shroud of Marin," *The New Yorker*, August 29, 2005, pp. 50–63.
15. Young, *Respectable Burial*, p. 161.
16. Ibid., p. 180.
17. Arbor Memorial Services, *Annual Information Form for the Year Ended October 31, 2004*.
18. John Heimbecker, "Final Purchase, Growing Demand: The Canadian Funeral Services Industry," Analytical Paper Series, Statistics Canada, 1995.

CHAPTER 4
1. Wirthlin Worldwide, *Executive Summary Of The Funeral And Memorial Information Counsel Study Of American Attitudes Toward Ritualization And Memorialization: 1999 Update.*, p. 3.
2. Erick Larson, "Fight to the Death: A battle between rival funeral-home dynasties puts the spotlight on a vast but quiet transformation in the way we bury our dead," *Time Magazine*, December 9, 1996.
3. Gary Bolton, personal correspondence to the author, March 21, 2007; Arbor Memorial Services, *2007 Annual Information Form for the Year Ended October 31, 2006*, p. 4.

4. Robert Bryce, "The dying giant," Salon.com, 1999, http://www.salon.com/news/feature/1999/09/29/sci, accessed November 27, 2005; CBC, *Marketplace*, "Inside the big business of funerals," broadcast January 16, 2002, http://www.cbc.ca/consumers/market/files/services/funerals, accessed January 16, 2006; Stuart C. Gilson, *Creating Value Through Corporate Restructuring: Case Studies in Bankruptcies, Buyouts, and Breakups*, John Wiley, 2001, pp. 30–31; Larson, "Fight to the Death."

5. Miriam Horn, "The Deathcare Business," *U.S. News and World Report*, March 3, 1998.

6. "SCI: A necessary societal role, A proud profession, A profitable enterprise," http://www.prnewswire.com/cnoc/SCIfun.html, accessed January 11, 2006.

7. Gilson, *Creating Value*, pp. 28–29.

8. Cited in Drew Cottle and Angela Keys, "The monopolisation of the Australian funeral industry?" *Journal of Australian Political Economy*, 54 (December 2004), p. 33.

9. Ibid., p. 34.

10. Cottle and Keys, "The monopolisation of the Australian funeral industry?" pp. 35–36.

11. Horn, "The Deathcare Business."

12. Bryce, "The dying giant."

13. Office of New York Attorney General Elliot Spitzer, "AG settles NYC funeral home monopoly case," http://www.oag.state.ny.us/press/1999/nov/nov17a_99.html, November 17, 1999.

14. Peter Franceschina and Rafael A. Olmeda, "$100 million settlement OK'd in Menorah grave desecrations," *South Florida Sun-Sentinel*, December 3, 2003.

15. Peter Franceschina, "Menorah Gardens charges dismissed $1 million fine in deal protects $100 million class action settlement," *South Florida Sun-Sentinel*, April 2, 2004.

16. Jim Greer, "Investors bury funeral giant: Compensation pacts, cemetery probe in Florida rattle SCI," *Houston Business Journal*, April 26, 2002; Paul Carson, "Florida Jewish community incensed as news of cemetery scandal breaks," *JTA*, December 27, 2001, http://www.jta.org/page_view_story.asp?intarticleid=10711&intcategoryid=4, accessed on September 9, 2006.

17. Alberta Funeral Services Regulatory Board, "Wayne Gorniak Fined $5,750," December 2005. Deborah Tetley, "Calgary funeral home under scrutiny: Province seizes cremation documents," *Calgary Herald*, August 15, 2003; Deborah Tetley, "Funeral firm charged; Cremation complaints sparked probe," *Calgary Herald*, September 25, 2003.

18. R. Robin McDonald, "Crematory's 'Unspeakable Disrespect' on Trial," www.law.com/jsp/article.jsp?id=1078368921591, accessed September 13, 2006.

19. Larson, "Fight to the Death."

20. Jonathan Harr, "The Burial," *The New Yorker*, November 1, 1999, pp. 70–95; Larson, "Fight to the Death."

21. Harr, "The Burial"; Larson, "Fight to the Death."

22. Gilson, *Creating Value*, p. 32, citing Kenneth Bagnell, "A Profitable Undertaking," *Globe and Mail*, October 21, 1988.

23. Harr, "The Burial"; Larson, "Fight to the Death."

24. Harr, "The Burial."
25. Ibid.; Larson, "Fight to the Death."
26. Larson, "Fight to the Death."
27. Harr, "The Burial"; Larson, "Fight to the Death."
28. David Barston and Monica Davey, "Anatomy of a swindle: The Rev. Henry J. Lyons and the Loewen Group," *St. Petersburg Times*, August 30, 1998.
29. Harr, "The Burial"; Larson, "Fight to the Death."
30. Barston and Davey, "Anatomy of a swindle."
31. Barston and Davey, "Anatomy of a swindle."
32. Gilson, *Creating Value*, p. 35.
33. Ibid., p. 36.
34. Ibid., p. 25.
35. Greer, "Investors bury funeral giant."
36. Bryce, "The dying giant."
37. Greer, "Investors bury funeral giant."
38. "Funeral home giants forced to retrench. Chains that spent freely to acquire assets now find themselves in a cash crunch," *Financial Post*, March 18, 2004.
39. "Two Funeral Giants to Make Deal to Merge," *New York Times*, April 3, 2006.
40. Young, *Respectable Burial*, p. 189.
41. Canada, "Amalgamation of Alderwoods Group, Inc. with a Wholly-Owned Subsidiary of Service Corporation International," Competition Bureau Canada, November 10, 2006, http://www.competitionbureau.gc.ca/internet/index.cfm?itemID=2235&lg=e, accessed April 5, 2007.
42. Seth Lubove, "Six Feet Under: Is Batesville Casket deviously fixing prices and gouging the bereaved? Or is it just a tough company protecting the channel?" *Forbes*, October 31, 2005.
43. Casket and Funeral Supply Association of America, "About the casket industry," Casket and Funeral Supply Association of America, http://www.cfsaa.org/about.php, accessed on January 30, 2006.
44. Lubove, "Six Feet Under."
45. Ibid.
46. *Funeral Consumers Alliance, Inc. et al. v. Service Corporation International et al.* (2004), at p. 10.
47. John R. Wilke, "Funeral industry is hit with casket-pricing suit," *The Wall Street Journal*, May 4, 2005.
48. Cited in *Funeral Consumers Alliance, Inc. et al. v. Service Corporation International et al.* (2004), at pp. 14–15.
49. Cited in David E. Harrington, "Breathing Life into the Funeral Market," *Regulation*, Spring 2003, p. 14.
50. Cited in *Funeral Consumers Alliance, Inc. et al. v. Service Corporation International et al.* (2004), at pp. 22–23.
51. Alton F. Doody, Jr., *Reinventing Funeral Service*, Centre for Advanced Funeral Management, 1995, p. 27.
52. Ibid., p. 32.
53. Ibid., p. 47.
54. Ibid., p. 48.
55. Ibid., pp. 61–62.

CHAPTER 5

1. Laderman, *Rest in Peace*, pp. 119–120
2. Eric Hobsbawm, "Introduction: Inventing Traditions," in *The Invention of Tradition*, Eric Hobsbawm and Terence Ranger (eds.), Cambridge University Press, 1983.
3. Timothy Taylor, *The Buried Soul: How Humans Invented Death*, Beacon Press, 2002, p. 4.
4. Ibid., pp. 13–27, 128, 229–233.
5. David Cannadine, "The Context, Performance and Meaning of Ritual: The British Monarchy and the 'Invention of Tradition' 1820–1977," in *The Invention of Tradition*, pp. 117–118.
6. Gayle E. O'Neill, "The Chemical Components of Cremated Remains," http://www.cremationassociation.org/html/for_consumers.html, accessed on February 17, 2007.
7. Emma Cook, "Saying goodbye our way," *The Guardian*, August 19, 2006.
8. BBC, "Crematoria warned over mercury," http://news.bbc.co.uk/1/hi/health/4160895.stm, accessed on August 23, 2006 [January 10, 2005].
9. Promessa, "Cremation," http://www.promessa.se/kremering_en.asp, accessed on August 22, 2006.
10. Paul Rahill, "Environmental Journey," http://www.cremationassociation.org/html/environment.html.
11. Appeal to the Environmental Appeal Board under section 44 of the *Waste Management Act*, http://www.eab.gov.bc.ca/waste/98was03a.htm, accessed on August 23, 2006.
12. Tara Carman, "Residents upset by crematorium soot," *Globe and Mail*, February 22, 2007.
13. Doug Ward, "Put a lid on fumes from cremation," *Vancouver Sun*, May 12, 2006.
14. For information on the Natural Death Centre, see http://www.ac026.dial.pipex.com/naturaldeath/index.html, accessed on March 30, 2006.
15. Paul Brown, "Green revolution waged after death," *The Guardian*, April 17, 2000.
16. Friend, "The Shroud of Marin."
17. For information on Kinkaraco, see http://www.kinkaraco.com/shrouds.html, accessed on August 14, 2006.
18. Michael Salisbury, *From My Death may Life Come Forth: A Feasibility Study of the Woodland Cemetery in Canada*, University of Guelph, School of Landscape Architecture, 2002.
19. For more information on the Natural Burial Cooperative, see http://www.naturalburial.ca.
20. Carolyn Heiman, "Saanich cemetery planning a 'green burial' site," *Victoria Times Colonist*, February 19, 2007.
21. Kate Connolly, "Sweden's new funeral rite," *The Telegraph*, September 28, 2005.
22. Memorial Society of Northern Ontario, http://www.memorialsociety.ca/, accessed August 16, 2006.
23. Memorial Society of British Columbia, http://www.memorialsocietybc.org/, accessed September 7, 2006.

CHAPTER 6

1. CBC, "Winnipeg family shocked by funeral home experience," http://www.cbc. ca/canada/manitoba/story/2007/02/08/wpg-funeral.html, accessed February 22, 2007.
2. CBC, "B.C. funeral industry feud may bump up costs," http://www.cbc.ca/ consumer/story/2006/09/06/funeral-society.html, accessed on September 7, 2006.
3. Quoted in Laderman, *Rest in Peace*, p. 81.
4. "FTC Proposes Funeral Practice Rule," *Federal Trade Commission News*, August 28, 1975, cited in Laderman, *Rest in Peace*, p. 134.
5. "Giving Undertakers Something to Cry About," *Business Week*, October 6, 1975, pp. 93–94, cited in Laderman, *Rest in Peace*, p. 135.
6. Laderman, *Rest in Peace*, pp. 135, 182.
7. Prothero, *Purified by Fire*, p. 174.
8. On August 12, 2006, I sent the following email to Arbor Memorial:
   "In your booklet Scattering: What you need to know before completing this irreversible act you state 'At a time of heightened emotion, the idea of Scattering may become romanticized, but in reality psychologists have found that people often discover a need later on for an accessible and identifiable 'place to go' as they come to terms with their grief in the months and years ahead.' Could you refer me to the psychological studies that this is based on?"
   I never received a response, even though I re-sent the message on December 27, 2006.
9. Memorial Gardens Canada, *Scattering: What You Need to Know Before Completing this Irreversible Act*, Memorial Gardens Canada, p. 2.
10. Economic and Social Research Council, http://www.esrcsocietytoday.ac.uk/ ESRCInfoCentre/ViewAwardPage.aspx?AwardId=3246, accessed on September 1, 2006.
11. Jenny Hockey, personal communication, August 29, 2006.
12. Arbor Memorial Services, *Annual Information Form for the Year Ended October 31, 2004*, p. 9.

PART TWO: FUNERAL PLANNING IN THE AGE OF CORPORATE DEATHCARE

1. Young, *Respectable Burial*, p. 136.

CHAPTER 7

1. Wirthlin Worldwide, *Executive Summary*, p. 3.
2. Cited in Penny Colman, *Corpses, Coffins, and Crypts: A History of Burial*, Henry Holt, 1997, pp. 131–132.

CHAPTER 8

1. Humber College, http://postsecondary.humber.ca/07321.htm, accessed August 25, 2006.
2. British Columbia Work Futures, http://www.workfutures.bc.ca/profiles/profile. cfm?print=true&lang=en&site=graphic&noc=6272, accessed on August 10, 2006.

3. Saskatchewan Job Futures, http://saskjobfutures.ca/profiles/profile.cfm?lang=en&site=txt&noc=6272, accessed August 10, 2006.

4. John Heimbecker, "Final Purchase, Growing Demand: The Canadian Funeral Services Industry," Analytical Paper Series, Statistics Canada, 1995.

5. Ibid.; Michelle Roterman, *Canada's Funeral Services Industry in the 1990s*, Statistics Canada, Services Industries Division, 2001.

6. Quebec, *What to do in the Event of Death*, Services Quebec, 2005, p. 10.

7. Ontario Board of Funeral Services, *Arranging a Funeral: What You Need to Know*, Ontario Board of Funeral Services, 2005.

8. Mark Harris, *Grave Matters: Journey Through the Modern Funeral Industry to a Natural Way of Burial*, Scribner, 2007, p. 119.

CHAPTER 9

1. Donald Grande and David S. Mezebish, "Skin Grafting," http://www.emedicine.com/derm/topic867.htm, accessed on June 18, 2006.

2. Kenneth V. Iserson, *Death to Dust: What Happens to Dead Bodies?* Galen Press, 1994, p. 53.

3. J.S. Gill, "Preliminary Statistics on Organ Donation, Transplantation and Waiting List: 2005 Preliminary Report," *Canadian Organ Replacement Register*, March 18, 2005.

4. Health Canada, "Organ Donation," Health Canada, 2001, http://www.hc-sc.gc.ca/ahc-asc/media/nr-cp/2001/2001_36bk1_e.html, accessed January 19, 2006.

5. Neil M. Lazar, Sam Shemie, George C. Webster and Bernard M. Dickens, "Bioethics for clinicians: 24. Brain death," *Canadian Medical Association Journal*, March 20, 2001.

6. Manitoba, *Vital Statistics Act*, http://www.canlii.org/mb/laws/sta/v-60/20060614/whole.html, accessed on August 9, 2006.

7. Michael Potts, *Canadian Medical Association Journal*, August 7, 2001, p. 269.

8. Greg A. Knoll and John E. Mahoney, "Non-heart-beating organ donation in Canada: Time to proceed?" *Canadian Medical Association Journal*, August 19, 2003, pp. 302–303.

9. Graeme M. Rocker, "Organ and tissue donation in the intensive care unit," *Canadian Medical Association Journal*, November 26, 2002, pp. 1248–1249.

10. C.J. Doig, "Is the Canadian health care system ready for donation after cardiac death? A note of caution," *Canadian Medical Association Journal*, October 10, 2006, pp. 905–906; Wayne Kondro, "Fragmented organ donation programs hinder progress," *Canadian Medical Association Journal*, October 24, 2006.

11. Health Canada, "Organ Donation.

12. Gill, "Preliminary Statistics."

13. David Baxter and Jim Smerdon, *Donation Matters: Demographics and Organ Transplants in Canada, 2000 to 2040*, The Urban Future Institute, 2000; Ian Hacking, "Whose body is it?" *London Review of Books*, December 14, 2006.

14. Mary Roach, *Stiff: The Curious Life of Human Cadavers*, Norton, 2003.

15. Annie Cheney, *Body Brokers: Inside the Underground Trade in Human Remains*, Broadway Books, 2006.

16. Royce McGillivray, "Body-Snatching in Ontario," *Canadian Bulletin of Medical*

History, 1988, pp. 51–60.

17. Jane Wildgoose, "Who really owns our bodies?" *The Guardian*, January 30, 2001, http:society.guardian.co.uk/alderhey/comment/0,8006,431006,00.html, accessed July 3, 2006.

18. Cronin, *Grave Exodus*; Anna M. Mayer, "The case of the body snatchers," *The Proceedings of the 9th Annual History of Medicine Days 2000*, W.A. Whitelaw (ed.), Faculty of Medicine University of Calgary, 2000, pp. 120–125; McGillivray, "Body-Snatching in Ontario"; Young, *Respectable Burial*.

19. University of Manitoba, *Service After Death: Information on Leaving One's Body For Anatomical Studies*, University of Manitoba, Department of Human Anatomy and Cell Science, 2006.

20. Ibid.

CHAPTER 10

1. Quebec, *What to do in the Event of Death*, p. 10.

2. *Saying Farewell: A helpful guide with information and forms to assist you through the death and dying process*, 3rd edition, Alberta Seniors and Community Supports, 2005, p. 13.

3. Canada, Office of Consumer Affairs, http://www.strategis.gc.ca/epic/internet/inoca-bc.nsf/en/ca01492e.html, accessed on June 8, 2006.

4. Manitoba, Workplace Safety and Health Division, "Formaldehyde Exposures in the Funeral Industry," http://www.gov.mb.ca/labour/safety/formaldehyde.html, accessed on August 18, 2006.

5. Kenneth V. Iserson, *Death to Dust: What Happens to Dead Bodies?* Galen Press, 1994, pp. 185–200; Darryl J. Roberts, *Profits of Death: An Insider Exposes the Death Care Industries*, Five Star Publications, 1997, pp. 11–29.

6. Casket and Funeral Supply Association of America, "About the casket industry," http://www.cfsaa.org/about.php, accessed on January 30, 2006.

7. Batesville Casket Company, http://www.batesville.com/materials_bronze.htm, accessed on February 3, 2006.

8. Batesville Casket Company, http://www.batesville.com/products.htm, accessed on February 3, 2006.

9. Casket and Funeral Supply Association of America, "About the casket industry."

10. Batesville Casket Company, http://www.batesville.com/materials_bronze.htm, accessed on February 3, 2006.

11. Wilbert Funeral Services, http://www.wilbertonline.com, accessed on January 31, 2006.

12. Ian Urbina, "In online mourning, don't speak ill of the dead," *New York Times*, November 5, 2006.

13. Friend, "The Shroud of Marin."

14. Cremation Association of North America, "Canadian Cremation Figures," http://www.cremationassociation.org/html/statistics.html, accessed on August 9, 2006.

15. Promessa, "Cremation," http://www.promessa.se/kremering_en.asp, accessed on August 22, 2006.

16. Canada, Office of Consumer Affairs, http://www.strategis.gc.ca/epic/internet/

inoca-bc.nsf/en/ca01492e.html, accessed on June 8, 2006.

17. Quebec, *What to do in the Event of Death*, p. 10

18. Alberta, *Saying Farewell: A Helpful Guide with Information and Forms to Assiost You through the Death and Dying Process*, Alberta Seniors and Community Supports 2005, 16

19. Ontario Board of Funeral Services, *Arranging a Funeral*, p. 3.

20. Chapel Lawn Memorial Gardens & Funeral Home, *Personal Tributes Brochure.*

21. Riverside Cemetery, http://www.riversidecemetery.com/pages.faq/terminology. html, accessed on August 21, 2006.

CHAPTER 11

1. Ernest Morgan, *Dealing Creatively with Death: A Manual for Death Education and Simple Burial*, Upper Access, 2001, p. 78.

2. Jeffrey Zaslow, "Some Get Carried Away Amid Frequent Eulogies," *Wall Street Journal*, July 11, 2003.

3. For information on Natural Endings, see http://www.naturalendings.co.uk/football-funerals.htm, accessed March 25, 2007.

4. Camille Bains, "Celebrant offers unique, personal funeral service," Canadian Press, August 9, 2006,

CHAPTER 12

1. Ontario Board of Funeral Services, *Prearranging a Funeral: What You Need to Know*, Ontario Board of Funeral Services, 2005.

2. Prince Edward Island Office of the Attorney General, *Prearranged Funeral Services Act*.

3. Ontario Board of Funeral Services, *Prearranging a Funeral*.

4. Arbor Memorial Services. *Annual Information Form for the Year Ended October 31, 2004*, p. 8.

5. Ontario Board of Funeral Services, *Prearranging a Funeral*.

6. For information on Assurant Solutions, see http://www.assurantpre-need.com/ ap/assurantpre-need/funeralplan/faq.htm, accessed on August 2, 2006.

7. Arbor Memorial Services, *Annual Information Form for the Year Ended October 31, 2004*, p. 8.

8. Everest Funeral Package, LLC, "Reviving a Dying Business," http://www.everestfuneral.com/pr-release-spring-2003.html, accessed on August 18, 2006.

9. Ibid.

10. Cara Williams, "Finances in the golden years," in *Perspectives on Labour and Income*, Vol. 4, No. 11, Statistics Canada, 2003, pp. 5–12.

11. Newfoundland and Labrador Auditor General, *Report of the Auditor General to the Provincial Assembly*, http://www.ag.gov.nl.ca/ag/2002Summary/booklet.htm, accessed on August 12, 2006.

12. Michelle Roterman, *Canada's Funeral Services Industry in the 1990s*, Statistics Canada, Services Industries Division, 2001.